Healing Crystals and Gemstones

from Amethyst to Zircon

Dr. Flora Peschek-Böhmer / Gisela Schreiber

KONECKY&KONECKY

Konecky & Konecky
72 Ayers Point Rd.
Old Saybrook, CT 06475

Copyright © 2002, W. Ludwig Buchverlag,
a division of Econ Ullstein List Verlag GmbH & Co.
Munich, Germany

English translation © 2003, Konecky & Konecky

English translation by Rosetta International and Sibylle Dausien

ISBN: 1-56852-442-0

All photos courtesy of Irmin Eitel, Munich with the exception of:
AKG, Berlin: 6,7; Bildarchiv Steffens, Mainz: 9, 17, 20 (Bridgeman Art Library);
Look, Munich: 10 (Jürgen Richter), 11 (Bernhard Edmaier);
Sudwest-Verlag, Munich: 46 (Ingolf Hatz)

Illustrations by Roger Kausch

NOTE FROM THE PUBLISHER
Any information given in this book is not intended to be taken as a replacement for medical advice. Any person with a condition requiring medical attention should consult a qualified physician or practitioner.

Printed in China

Contents

The Healing Power

of Crystals

and

Gemstones

Stones come in all different colors and shades and in different crystal structures. That explains their various healing effects. Learn how to recognize and use the power of healing stones.

Healing Stones in Mythology and History

All gemstones have one thing in common: they originate from the hot magma, of which the inside of the earth is composed. Thousands of years cooling, gradual movement and displacement have formed stones, rocks and even high mountains. This continuous process of geologic change causes rocks and minerals of various kinds to come into being. They are formed from dust, sand, chemical substances and invisible acids that have dissolved in water.

From the very infancy of the human race, gemstones have exercised a powerful fascination. The therapeutic use of gems is not a new or alternative healing method. The art of healing with stones is thousands of years old. Evidence that gemstones were used to heal disease can be found from the most ancient civilizations. They were also considered to have protective and talismanic properties and to keep evil spirits away. Shamans and medicine men harnessed the power of crystals in ceremonies and rituals. This ancient knowledge has been passed down to our day.

A stone's healing power depends upon a number of factors: how it is recovered, whether it comes into contact with acids or liquids in which crystals can grow.

The earliest reports of gems' healing properties date as far back as the fourth millennium before Christ. They can be found in Sumerian writings and the transcriptions from Indian vedic texts. In the Vedic tradition naturopathic medicine was known as Ayurveda, a word that derives from sanskrit "ayur" meaning life and "veda" meaning wisdom. Ayurveda describes in detail how to prepare elixirs, pastes and powders made from gemstones. Doctors in India would place colored gemstones on the painful areas of their patients' bodies and, to enhance their healing power, use them as channels for the light and warmth of the sun. Knowledge of these ancient practices had for a time been all but lost, but today it again forms part of the medical curriculum in Indian universities.

In the first Chinese medical book, written 5000 years ago by Shen Nung, the Red Emperor, can be found detailed descriptions of gemstones and their influence on the human body.

Stones in the Bible

Further evidence of the significance attributed to gemstones can be found in the many references to them in the Bible. They often serve as symbols for health and godliness. The twelve tribes of Israel are represented by twelve corresponding precious stones placed in the breastplate of Israel's high priest. The stones are to be arranged in four rows of

The great mystic of the Middle Ages, Hildegard von Bingen, devoted much thought to the healing power of stones.

Hildegard von Bingen employed many stones whose healing or protective virtues are referred to in Holy Scripture.

three stones. According to later tradition they possessed extraordinary powers.

In John's vision of the New Jerusalem in Revelation, the heavenly city is built from gemstones.

And the building of the wall of it was of jasper: and the city was pure gold, like unto clear glass. And the foundations of the wall of the city were garnished with all manner of precious stones. The first foundation was jasper; the second, sapphire; the third, a chalcedony; the fourth, an emerald; the fifth, sardonyx; the sixth, sardius; the seventh, chrysolyte; the eighth, beryl; the ninth, a topaz; the tenth, a chrysoprasus; the eleventh, a jacinth; the twelfth, an amethyst. And the twelve gates were twelve pearls; every several gate was of one pearl: and the street of the city was pure gold, as it were transparent glass.

(Rev 21:18-21)

The number twelve was a sign of the highest harmony and perfection. The strength of the stones were directly attributed to the power of God. The twelve walls of Jerusalem, the twelve apostles and the twelve signs of the zodiac all had corresponding gems, each with its own special qualities.

Healing Stones in Antiquity and the Middle Ages

Every advanced, ancient civilization knew of the healing properties of crystals and stones. Whether in leather pouches as carried by the Sumerians, or worn as talismans and amulets, or distilled into powders or elixirs, gemstones were known by natural healers to strengthen those who wore them and protect them from evil spirits, sickness and disaster. The Greek philosopher Aristotle spoke of the power of healing stones. The Romans carried cut stones with them to ward off sickness and bad luck. The Egyptians wore amulets made of amethyst, hematite, jasper, carnelian or lapis lazuli. Often the stones were polished or hammered into scarabs, symbols of creation, and accompanied the dead to protect them in their next life.

Throughout the ancient world gems were used to treat many of the same ailments, but the modalities of treatment varied among different cultures. Famous Greek, Roman and Arabic doctors and scholars wrote of their power, and they played an important role in their methods of healing. These early doctors mixed them with plant extracts, heated or pulverized them or treated them with chemicals.

After the flourishing of the healing arts in antiquity, the art of healing with stones was revived in the Middle Ages. Isidore of Seville, Konrad von

Megenberg, Albertus Magnus and the Benedictine, Marbod, Bishop of Rennes, all wrote of their efficacy. Marbod's little handbook, *Liber lapidum seu de gemmis*, provided an overview of sixty gems and their therapeutic properties. For its time, the book was a bestseller. It was translated into four languages and went through fourteen editions from 1511 to 1799.

The *Physika* of Hildegard von Bingen

A work of the twelfth century by Hildegard von Bingen (1098-1179), the *Physika*, dealt with gemstones in a comprehensive fashion. Both an abbess and a mystic, Hildegard developed entirely new ways of healing with gems, which were one of the pillars of her medical system. She realized that medicine needed a holistic orientation and that physical and spiritual disorders could not be isolated from environmental influences. The phases of the moon, inadequacies in diet and bad habits of living were as important to recognize in the determination of treatment as the patient's constitution and psychological state. Accordingly, the methods of treatment varied widely: some diseases called for a change in lifestyle, others were treated with herbs, powders, pastes and natural essences, all of which had to be carefully balanced one with another. Stones were placed on parts of the patient's anatomy and charged with energy. Consumption of drinks and concoctions made of powdered minerals and the essences of gemstones were prescribed for specific illnesses.

When Paracelsus was alive one could buy gemstones such as garnet, hyacinth, sapphire, ruby, topaz, emerald, fluorite, lapis lazuli, carnelian, rock crystal, and nephrite in apothecary shops.

The Teachings of Paracelsus

The most famous physician of the Renaissance was Theophrastus Bombastus von Hohenheim, better know as Paracelsus. More than anyone of his time, he delved into the healing properties of minerals and gems. In his work, *On Minerals*, he distinguished between chemical formulae and the elemental powers that reside within stones. According to his teachings, pulverized rocks were used to treat symptoms, while their essential force attacked the root causes of sickness and prevented their reoccurrence.

"There is only one source of health: the irresistible, wise, limitlessly powerful healer within us. This healer has the ability to cure all things. The only reason that someone becomes sick is that the inner healer has been weakened and obstructed through careless habits of living. When I want to treat a person, the only thing I attempt to do is to restore the healing power within."

(Paracelsus)

The scientific writings of Paracelsus (1493–1541) were groundbreaking studies for the future of medicine.

Fateful Gemstones

Precious stones have not always brought their owners health and happiness. Diamonds have had an especially checkered history, and there are stories about the grief that they have brought to their possessors. Just as diamonds reflect the light of all colors of the spectrum, so under certain circumstances they can mirror human passion and weakness.

Stones come in all colors with different crystal structures. Their healing powers are explained by the fact that stones like people are part of the natural order.

The Hope Diamond

No other stone has had as many dark tales associated with it as the Hope Diamond. Legend has it that the 112-karat sapphire-blue diamond originally served as the eye of a statue of the Hindu goddess Sita. It was stolen by a high Brahmin. His crime so angered the goddess that she laid a curse upon the diamond: unhappiness would follow all who dared to possess the stone.

In 1642, the stone mysteriously found its way into the possession of Jean-Baptiste Tavernier. He brought it from India to Europe, where it was fashioned into a heart shape. Tavernier sold the diamond, which was now only 67 carats, to a man named Toquet and then returned to India, where he was eaten by wild beasts. Toquet died wretchedly in the Bastille. The stone next passed to King Louis XIV. It is said that he only wore it once and soon after died of the pox. Louis XV apparently never touched the stone. Louis XVI and his wife, Marie Antoinette, could not resist its allure. They were both beheaded on the guillotine. During the French revolution the stone was stolen from the royal treasury and disappeared until 1830 when it turned up at a London dealer's. By that time the diamond had been whittled down further to 44 karats, the weight it has today.

The Hopes, a British banking family, were the only ones who escaped the full force of the curse. The wife of the second Lord Hope ran off with another man. And even though the cuckolded husband sold the stone, both he and his wife died in poverty. After that a Russian duke owned the diamond and gave it to his lover, a dancer with the Folies-Bergères. Jealousy drove him to shoot her, and he then was murdered. Other owners lost close relatives from poison, auto accidents and other tragic circumstances, and they themselves often met violent ends. Since 1958 the Hope Diamond has been housed at the Smithsonian Institute in Washington DC.

The Pitt or Regent Diamond

A slave found this 410-karat stone in a mine in South India in 1701. He thought it would be his means of escape, but a sailor murdered him in cold blood. A jewelry dealer sold it to the English statesman William Pitt. Pitt had the stone cut into a brilliant of 140.5 karats. After selling it in 1717 to the Duc d'Orleans, he hanged himself. In 1722, the stone was recarved to adorn the crown of King Louis XIV. Later Napoleon had it ornament the pommel of his sword. In 1887 the Regent Diamond was given to the Louvre, where it remains to this day.

To promote the film Breakfast at Tiffany's, *Audrey Hepburn wore the Tiffany Diamond at a public relations event.*

The Yellow Tiffany Diamond

This gemstone is one of the largest and most fascinating yellow diamonds in the world. It was found in 1887 in the Kimberley mines of South Africa. At that time it weighed 287.42 karats. It owes its name to Charles Lewis Tiffany, the founder of Tiffany's in New York, who purchased it in 1878. Tiffany carved it down to 128.54 karats. The diamond has 90 facets. Today the stone can be seen on the first floor of Tiffany's Fifth Avenue store.

The famous Hope Diamond has many dark stories associated with it.

The hard crust of the earth consists of many tectonic plates.

How Stones Come into Being

Over the course of billions of years the universe has been forming itself from the interaction of matter, energy, rotation and gravity. According to current scientific opinion, the earth began as a dust cloud that solidified through powerful gravitational effects. Countless particles comprising dust and gaseous elements were brought together by rotational forces to form the kernel of our planet.

Out of the Heat of the Earth

Particulate matter as well as larger bits of stone and metal that found themselves within the earth's magnetic field were drawn into and fed the increasing mass of the planet's center. The more massive it became the more compressed its entire structure. Centripetal acceleration heated the entire mass and created a giant molten fireball. Over an enormous stretch of time the fireball cooled down, and the hard surface of the planet was formed, containing the still burning fire within it. This fiery core of bubbling magma provides heat and energy to the earth to this day. In the magma reside the basic materials out of which crystals and stones are formed. All material that exists on the earth's surface also exists in liquid form within its core. As it cools and rises to the surface, it enters into new molecular combinations. Out of these processes come all of the varied mineral riches that we find in the world around us.

Where tectonic plates meet, fissures are created. Out of these, over time, arise high mountains.

The earth's crust seems fairly thick — about five kilometers under the ocean and anywhere between thirty and one hundred kilometers under continental land masses — but in comparison to the earth's diameter of 12,756 kilometers, it is a relatively thin coating. Below the surface the temperature gets hotter as one approaches the center. That we do not live on a planet made of solid rock becomes apparent when earthquakes or volcanic eruptions occur. Liquefied stone in the form of molten lava rises to the surface and cools to produce volcanic craters. In the case of volcanic eruptions, fractures or thin places in the earth crust, as for example at the boundaries of tectonic plates, allow the hot magma to erupt onto the surface.

Primary Stones

◆ **Magmatic rock** The first step in the formation of stone is always the cooling of the hot magma. The result of this cooling is called primary stone or magmatic rock. The cooling process causes crystals to form and grow. The composition of the magma is not, however, everywhere the same. This variation is the basis for the wide diversity in the structure of rocks and minerals. In addition, different forms can arise out of the same basic material. When crystals are composed out of one basic material they are called minerals; when they are formed from diverse materials they are called stones. Their composition depends upon the length and speed of the process of solidification.

◆ **Volcanic rock** The magma that is hurled onto the surface of the earth during volcanic eruptions cools relatively quickly; it forms itself into molten lava. When lava rises and condenses on the surface, the resultant crystallization process produces what is known as volcanic rock. As the cooling process usually happens quickly most volcanic stones are not very large. There is not sufficient time for large chains of crystal to form. Volcanic stones with healing properties include jasper and porphyry. Obsidian, volcanic glass, comes into being when crystals do not form during the cooling process.

◆ **Plutonic rock** Stone that remains buried within the earth's surface takes longer to cool. This kind of stone is called plutonic. Stones and minerals form out of liquid magma. The heavier elements sink, and the lighter ones rise to the surface. This explains why minerals and stones are found in layers. Through the movement of tectonic plates these substances deep within the planet find their way to the surface. Not all plutonic rocks crystallize directly in liquid magma. Some form from hot vapor and gas. Forced under great pressure through cracks and fissures, already formed crystals can lose some material and combine with other chemicals to produce new materials. This happens when gas condenses into water, which under great pressure can occur at a temperature of 375° centigrade. Stones formed in this fashion include agate, amethyst, rock crystal, chalcedony and rock quartz. They have the time and space to slowly cool and grow into their full beauty. Aventurine, olivine, rose quartz and zircon are all plutonic rocks with healing properties. Healing stones that originate out of the contact with water include amazonite, aragonite, fluorite, kunzite and moonstone.

A special form of volcanic rock is obsidian. It is created when lava cools very quickly, as, for example, when it flows into cold water.

Magma is the source of all minerals. It comprises all of the basic elements found on earth.

Secondary stones

The erosion of rocks and mountains is a slow but constant process. Rocks, stones and pebbles are dislodged and slide down into valleys. As they roll, slide and are washed down by streams, their surfaces are smoothed, and their size diminishes. Sand, dirt and particles of minerals that have been dissolved in water are collected in deeper strata of the earth and in river beds or in lake or ocean floors. This material, called sediment, enters into new combinations. Some of this material breaks apart and is reconstituted into new kinds of minerals. These new layers become denser and out of them new sedimentary stones are created.

The second step in the life of stones comes when primary stone reaches the surface. Here it encounters wind and weather. Water washes elements away, and freezing causes them to break apart.

The basic principle behind the secondary process of rock formation is easy to explain: existing stones get crushed by environmental factors. The resultant particles are scattered about and reform in new places. Calcite and pyrite are sedimentary stones with great healing properties.

Tertiary stones

The third phase of development – the composition of tertiary stones – is a further transformation from the before-mentioned processes. The constant movement of large rock masses creates areas of intense pressure. Rock layers are pressed into giant mountains or are pushed farther down into the earth. When two tectonic plates come into contact, one will rise to the top, and the larger of the two will be pushed to the bottom. In the lower levels there are higher temperatures and greater pressure on these layers of stone than in the upper levels. Certain chemical combinations and the weaker layers cannot withstand the heat and pressure and react by forming new structures that, for example, take up less space. Crystals are arranged in a parallel structure; adjacent minerals join together. Other minerals are completely destroyed or melt together in these furnace-like conditions.

Thus new stones are often harder and more resistant than the substances from which they originated. From the relatively soft chalk arises the much harder marble. This process is called metamorphosis; the stones that are thereby created are called metamorphic. When this metamorphic stone melts, it sinks deeper and produces new magma. Thus the circle of stone formation continues.

Recognizing Stones and Distinguishing between Them

Gemstones are most easily recognized by their color and luster. These qualities along with their brilliance and degree of transparency are their most distinctive characteristics.

Those who study gems also consider their crystal structure and degree of hardness as well as the workmanship that they display. There are certain guidelines that should be followed to be able to appreciate and evaluate gemstones.

The rare dioptase is a copper-based mineral and for that reason has a green tinge.

Color and Luster

The most striking quality of gemstones is their color. Often color is the deciding factor in the attraction a stone has for an individual. In most cases a stone's color depends upon its chemical composition and is directly linked to its healing properties. What we perceive as color variation derives from the refraction, diffraction, reflection and absorption of light rays. These physical phenomena arise from the composition and formation of the observed object.

For some stones, labeled idiochromatic, color inheres in their chemical structure. Most of these come in a single color, which is very pronounced. Malachite, pyrite, turquoise and hematite are stones of this kind. To discern the natural color of some gemstones, one needs to look at their streak. To do this, one scratches the unglazed surface of a porcelain plate with the edge of a stone. This will leave a thin streak of powder. If the stone is so hard that it can inscribe itself on glass, it first needs to be pulverized and then can be rubbed onto porcelain. If a streak still cannot be seen, then one has encountered a mineral that owes its color to the presence of foreign particles.

For minerals of this kind, called allochromatic, color derives from additional chemicals within their structure. Sometimes it is only a question of a small amount of different compounds, pigments, mineral structures or foreign atoms in pure minerals. Nonetheless, they are the source of the stone's color. Precious stones can exist in various colors. Variations in shade depend upon

Most mineral deposits are discovered by accident, but it also requires long experience in geology to find veins and lodes of precious stone.

the presence of chromium, iron, cobalt, manganese, nickel or silicon. For this reason it is difficult to identify a stone simply by its color. Depending upon the chemical composition, the same elements can produce different colors. So, for example, the presence of chromium makes rubies and spinels red, while it is responsible for the green color in emeralds. Tourmaline, jasper, apatite and beryl display vivid color variations. Because the nature of stones changes with their color, we call beryl bixbyite when it is red, aquamarine when blue and emerald when green.

In special cases radiation can affect a mineral's chemical composition and color. This process allows us today to artificially change or enhance a mineral's color. Diamonds, for example, can display all of the different nuances of blue and green, yellow and brown when subjected to the effects of radiation. By irradiating rock crystal one produces smoky quartz. Because this manipulation is not comparable to natural formative processes, one must bear in mind that it can alter or even nullify a stone's healing properties.

Through the effect of natural radiation from the earth's mantle, the color of stones can change, just as film is changed through exposure to light.

Fissures, veins and inclusions are all responsible for the refraction of light. Just as in a prism light is broken into all of the colors of the spectrum, so a crystal's form and arrangement determine the reflection and play of light. Labradorite, for example, is lamellate in form, and light passing through it creates an iridescent effect. When light is broken up by tiny veins in minerals, as is the case with star sapphire and star ruby, it gives the stone a star-like radiance. Opal owes its shining color to microscopic drops of water that are trapped beneath its surface.

Small pockets of gas can make stones shimmer, as, for example, rainbow obsidian. Some stones produce their own light. When these stones are subjected to heat or ultraviolet light they emit a colored radiance. This quality is called luminescence and is of particular value in the identification of stones.

The Seven Crystal Forms

A crystal consists of a three-dimensional arrangement of atomic particles, the crystal lattice. Each type of gemstone has its own chemical structure, which accounts for the crystal's shape. The juxtaposition of angles in its outer form reflects its internal atomic structure. Even when a crystal develops through distortion or displacement and does not maintain its pure form, its structural angles remain the same. Stones can be categorized into seven basic forms.

♦ Cubic
♦ Trigonal
♦ Hexagonal
♦ Tetragonal
♦ Orthorhombic
♦ Monoclinic
♦ Triclinic

The beauty of crystals' geometry has always been admired. The term crystal comes from Greek word, krystallos, meaning ice.

Some stones do not form crystal lattices; these are called amorphous. In this class are a number of precious stones that originate from organic substances such as pearl, amber or coral, but opal and obsidian are also included in this category. No matter what the size or color of a crystal, its structure always remains the same. For example, jasper, be it red, brown, yellow or green always has a trigonal structure.

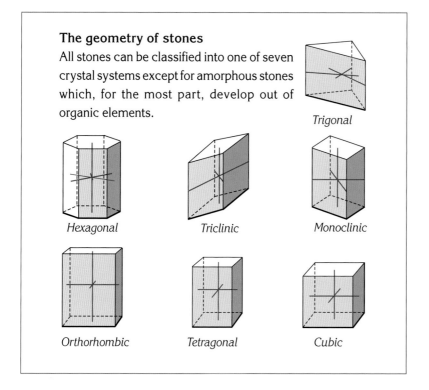

The geometry of stones
All stones can be classified into one of seven crystal systems except for amorphous stones which, for the most part, develop out of organic elements.

Trigonal

Hexagonal   Triclinic   Monoclinic

Orthorhombic   Tetragonal   Cubic

Degrees of Hardness

One essential difference between various stones is their degree of hardness. By definition each gemstone can scratch a softer stone and can in turn be scratched by a harder stone. The degree of hardness has been measured for over two centuries by the scale devised by an Austrian professor of mineralogy, Friedrich Mohs. The Mohs scale classifies stones from the softest, 1, to the hardest, 10. Diamond is the hardest stone, the softest are gypsum and soapstone, also called talc.

Some stones are soft enough to be broken in one's bare hands; others are so hard that glass cannot cut them.

Transparency and Refraction of Light

The transparency of gemstones varies considerably with different colors. For every shade there are clear, semi-transparent and matte stones. Rock crystal and topaz are clear and transparent. They comprise all the colors of the rainbow and possess great healing power.

The Mohs scale		
Hardness	**Characteristics**	**Stone**
1	Can be scratched with fingernail	Gypsum, soapstone
2	Also can be scratched with fingernail	Rock salt
3	Can be scratched with knife or coin	Calcite
4	Can be carved with knife or glass	Fluorite
5	Can be carved with a knife	Apatite
6	Can be carved with glass or steel pen	Orthoclase
7	Can scratch glass	Quartz
8	Can scratch glass and quartz	Topaz
9	Can scratch topaz and glass, and can itself be scratched only by diamond	Corundum (blue = sapphire, red = ruby)
10	Cannot itself be scratched, but can scratch all other gemstones	Diamond

Transparency

A bright, transparent stone can, depending upon its crystal formation and the way in which it is cut, break up light rays and display all of the colors of the rainbow. But the transparency of a particular mineral is not always the same. The smallest cracks or inclusions can make them cloudy and translucent. Just as the presence of foreign elements lend different colors to the same crystals, so there can be different levels of transparency for these stones. They can range from transparent to opaque. The size of its crystals also will influence the transparency of stone.

Luster

Basically there are three categories of luster: metallic, semi-metallic and non-metallic. These labels, however, can at times become misleading, since matte minerals are also considered to be non-metallic. In the metallic class belong opaque, ore-bearing stones that strongly reflect light, such as pyrite. The most pronounced degree of non-metallic luster can be found in transparent minerals with high refractive indices. This is called adamantine (diamond-like) luster, after that come vitreous, or glassy, luster, greasy luster and finally stones with dull luster.

Cutting

The art of working on gemstones and jewelry was practiced in ancient Egypt and India to intensify the sparkle and color of these precious objects. Various techniques of cutting have been perfected from a simple step cut, to complex fashioning of many surfaces. The brilliant cut was developed in the seventeenth century, primarily to bring out the maximum brilliance of diamonds. Through cutting one can achieve symmetrical, smooth surfaces as well as facets and crowns. Facetted stones increase the refraction of light intensifying their color. In this way, one can so enhance the sparkle of transparent stones that they can display all the colors of the rainbow. This accounts for the "fire" in gemstones.

Non-transparent stones are mostly cut with smooth, curved surfaces. In the trade these cuts are called cabochon. Soft stones can only be cut in this fashion; no other way is possible. For this

The cut of a diamond accounts for its value and its individual character, as in the Agra Diamond shown here.

Minerals have different degrees of transparency and kinds of luster. Through cutting techniques the refraction of light is intensified, giving gemstones their "fire".

reason soft stones are tumbled or worked into beads or ovals for necklaces, brooches or rings. It is important to note that the form and the workmanship lavished on a gemstone can have a definite effect on its healing power.

There is a simple way of measuring the weight of gemstones. Weight is specified in carats (1 carat = .02 grams). To be truly valuable a stone must meet certain requirements. Most important is its size and the absence of flaws. The purity and rarity of the mineral also needs to be taken into account. Not of least importance is the workmanship that has gone into it. Here the cutting and shaping of the stone are most important. This will bring out the perfection of a true gemstone.

Workmanship not only affects the aesthetic quality of a gemstone. It can also make a difference to it healing power.

Forms of Gemstones

Gemstones are divided in to three categories: rough stones, those subjected to simple fashioning and those showing complex workmanship. In general healing stones always have an aesthetic component, which makes them valuable in themselves. Finally there are precious and semi-precious stones that are used in jewelry. Buying gemstones is a matter of trust. It is important to find a reliable jeweler or mineral dealer, who can advise you. Healing stones work slowly. Neither time nor faith in their powers are factors in the effectiveness of healing stones. It doesn't matter whether or not you believe in their power. The stones will have an influence on the body. But those who are more sensitive will experience their effects more quickly and intensely.

Rough stones, such as sardonyx, can be made into jewelry or touchstones.

Rough Stones – Primordial Magic

Every rough stone is unique. Taken from the living rock, they are allowed to remain in their natural condition. They are distinguished by their simplicity, as well as by their beauty and healing power. Free of the imprint of human workmanship, unbridled energy flows through them. For this reason rough stones possess the greatest healing power. It is recommended that they be placed directly upon the body.

◆ In a developing crystal all of the energy of is concentrated at its point. Crystals can be used to make pendulums, but these should only be used for therapeutic purposes following the guidance of an experienced practitioner.

♦ There are usually small pockets or holes in naturally developing crystals. Energy gathers in these pockets. These are used as storage areas when recharging a stone.

♦ Aggregate crystals have points that project in different directions. This disperses their power and can restore the balance of energy in their surroundings. They are also used to recharge other stones.

The value of stones increases when set in precious metals.

Tumbled stones – Gentle and Calming

Tumbled stones derive their name from they way in which they are made. Rough stones are put together with water and sand in a drum that is then turned. This abrades their points and edges, and one is left with rounded stones with smooth surfaces. Tumbled stones are often used as touchstones. Their strong vibrations produce a powerful healing influence. They are best suited to be laid or pressed onto the body. In nature one finds natural silicate stones in river beds. These have been rubbed smooth and round by the action of sand and water.

The rounded shape of these stones makes them ideal for placing on the body. By holding and rubbing these stones their energy passes through the hand, and the entire body becomes infused with their power. Flat tumbled stones can be placed under one's pillow or pressed directly onto a painful area of the body. Even when worn over clothing, they do not lose their effect. Hold one in your hand and feel its peaceful influence.

There are three forms of stones: rough stone, which has the greatest healing power, tumbled stone, mostly used for touchstones, and gemstones, which are made into jewelry.

Jewelry – The Healing Power of Beauty

Jewelry made from different stones can have a positive or negative effect. The precious metals in which they are set can increase their energy level. Skilled workmanship also increases the healing power. Gold settings will enhance the power of every stone. Silver strengthens the vibratory intensity of coral and turquoise. Single stones are best used in jewelry, especially as in this way they can always be worn on the body. Multiple stones should be worn as necklaces, armbands or on key rings. With the help of one experienced in the therapeutic art of stones, jewelry can be tailored for an individual's particular health needs.

Healing Gemstones and the Signs of the Zodiac

The magic of gemstones is closely bound up with astrology. According to astrological lore, gemstones are intermediaries between the macrocosm and the microcosm that resides within each of us. Find the stones that best correspond to your sign.

The Magical Connection between Star and Stone

From the earliest times, people in every culture have sought a way of connecting with the stars and discerning the effect they have on their destinies. According to astrological teachings the sign of the zodiac under which an individual is born has a great influence on his life, his soul, his character and his general health. Each sign has its own characteristic qualities; each corresponds to a specific area of the body and accounts for its strength or weakness. Particularly if one suffers from chronic ailments, one should look for gemstones that not only address symptoms, but also serve to support one's basic personality type and counteract its weaknesses.

Capricorn (December 22 – January 20)

For Capricorn no workload is too heavy, no career path too steep. He relies on his own will power to take him to the top. This sign combines ambition and endurance. Capricorns are realists through and through. While others are dreaming about what they might do with an increase in salary, Capricorn already has earned and sensibly invested it. He believes strongly in tradition. For him everything has to be just so. But because he takes things so seriously, he sometimes misses out on the enjoyment of life and jeopardizes relationships on account of business responsibilities and adherence to convention. Even so he is capable of deep and passionate feeling and can flourish in a long-term relationship. But before he can truly share his feelings with someone else, he will scrutinize that person to make sure that his trust and affection have not been misplaced.

Conscientiousness is more than just a word for Capricorn. He will do everything he can to fulfill his responsibilities on time and in the most careful fashion.

The main gemstones for Capricorn
◆ **Onyx** – For those born under the sign of Capricorn, onyx increases wisdom and serenity. It helps them in their striving towards ever higher goals and in their appreciation for the beautiful things in life. Onyx strengthens their sense of responsibility and helps them recognize conflicts early on.
◆ **Malachite** – Malachite can help Capricorns become aware of their deep unconscious wishes, dreams and feelings. If they can

allow a little more room for emotion, their success and satisfaction will be greater.

♦ **Tourmaline** – The dark green variety of tourmaline helps Capricorns achieve wealth and fame. It is a reminder that these are fair rewards for effort and hard work. But it also helps temper Capricorn's natural pride and arrogance.

♦ **Agate** – Agate helps Capricorn feel safe and relaxed. It is a most important remedy for those who cannot let go even with their own immediate family. In such cases agate will promote the ability to trust and let down one's guard.

♦ **Black pearl** – Black pearl has a calming effect on Capricorns. Even if they have had bitter experiences, it will help them to see that growth and understanding can come out of suffering. With black pearl Capricorn can discover the beauty and depth of his character.

♦ **Moss agate** – Moss agate is the lucky stone for Capricorn. It assures happiness in love. It enhances communication with friends and colleagues and provides a deeper connection with nature.

Strong emotions make Capricorn insecure and uneasy. He disguises these feelings behind a reserved and distant front.

Other important gemstones for Capricorn

♦ **Rock crystal** – Rock crystal helps those born under the sign of Capricorn achieve clarity and spiritual purity. In that way it helps them go beyond the confines of their expectations and loosen the grip of cares and responsibilities to enjoy a more expansive life.

♦ **Diamond** – Diamond strengthens the concentration of Capricorns. It helps them achieve their goals unhindered. It opens them up to worlds of art, music and beauty, allowing them to transcend day-to-day cares and take pleasure in the world around them.

♦ **Jasper** – Capricorns will find that this gemstone promotes steadfastness and self-confidence. At the same time, it will remind them that the search for meaning must extend beyond their everyday cares and duties.

♦ **Obsidian** – Obsidian will help Capricorns reach their goals. It protects them from negative influences and vibrations that can drain their life force. By recognizing the correspondences between microcosm and macrocosm, Capricorn can avoid emotional problems and achieve balance and stability.

♦ **Smoky quartz** – This mineral can help Capricorn loosen

attachment to material things and become more sensitive and understanding to those around them.

♦ **Sapphire** – Sapphire and smoky quartz work well together to help Capricorn recognize the ephemeral nature of the moment and learn to acknowledge the sacred principles guiding the cosmos.

♦ **Citrine** – Citrine strengthens Capricorn's aura and leads to self-confidence and warm-heartedness. It can help him through those difficult times, in which he wavers, and self doubt gains the upper hand. Then it can provide a sense of inner peace and the confidence to once again believe in life.

Aquarius (January 21 – February 19)

Aquarians possess cheerfulness and determination and strive for freedom and independence. They embrace change. For them that is the only way to progress. Aquarians can become technological innovators, political reformers, even revolutionaries. They have to accept that their thirst for knowledge and continual hungering after the new may alienate or even drive away some partners. They love intense discussion and debate and are generous, open-minded and tolerant. They can, however, allow their ideals and dreams to get the better of their sense of reality, thereby inviting a rude awaken-ing when hard, cold facts interfere with the accomplishment of what they hope to achieve. Partners do not always have an easy time of it with Aquarians, since their restless explorations can be an impediment to closeness and devotion between people.

Aquarius does not like to be confined by narrow systems, unless it is by his own choosing. They can create great physical and mental suffering for him.

The main gemstones for Aquarius

♦ **Turquoise** – This gemstone is effective in counteracting and moderating mood swings. It can help Aquarius temper the urge for new things and return to an appreciation of his partner and the realities of his situation. It can also help counter indifference, which is one of the negative qualities that Aquarians can display toward those nearest to them.

♦ **Aquamarine** – Aquamarine helps Aquarius achieve unity and psychological integration. It mediates between the desire for freedom and the need for boundaries. With its support Aquarius can maintain a sense of freedom in the midst of adversity and constraint.

*In his private life
Aquarius defies
convention.
Cheerful and
independent, he
goes his own way.*

◆ **Labradorite** – Labradorite strengthens Aquarians' intuition and helps them realize their goals. It calms their natural restlessness and provides inner composure. Black, Finnish labradorite is particularly effective in promoting fantasy and creativity. It also strengthens the powers of recall.

◆ **Amazonite** – For Aquarius this gemstone has a calming effect. It enhances vitality and enjoyment of life. It symbolizes an openness to one's environment and neighbors and thereby smoothes the way to fellowship and love. Amazonite is also effective in combating mood swings and strengthens the self-confidence of those who wear it. It also assuages some of the pain of grieving and promotes sound, healthful sleep.

◆ **Falcon's eye** – Falcon's eye stands for awareness. Its possessor begins to see the world and those around him with renewed clarity. It helps Aquarius to concentrate on essential things and address character weaknesses. It sharpens perceptions and provides an infusion of energy and freshness.

◆ **Topaz** – Topaz leads to self-realization. Most helpful is blue topaz; for Aquarius, it fosters creativity and the ability to actualize ideas and projects. All varieties of topaz provide their possessors with enhanced receptivity and a richer fantasy life.

◆ **Fluorite** – Fluorite can lead Aquarius to higher levels of understanding. It strengthens the intellectual apprehension of the truth and the grasp of cosmic ideas.

◆ **Malachite** - Malachite is very important for Aquarius. It can bring unconscious elements that have resided as vaguely formulated hopes or plans into the full light of awareness. It teaches Aquarius to believe in himself and listen to his own body. It also provides a brake on recklessness.

Other important gemstones for Aquarius

◆ **Jade** – Jade has ancient cultic associations. It helps bind Aquarius to tradition. It offers him an understanding and appreciation of perennially transmitted wisdom. Through its calming effect it can provide a pause for reflection that is sometimes an essential counterweight to the Aquarian's restless yearning after new experiences.

◆ **Chalcedony** – With its soothing influence and calming rays, chalcedony can assist those suffering from mood swings. It can help during times of personal and professional stress. It is a good corrective for impatience and restlessness and can impart serenity to those born under this sign.

◆ **Diamond** – Diamonds impart order to the sometimes overactive imagination of Aquarius. They can support efforts toward self-awareness and promote qualities of perseverance and emotional stability.

◆ **Moonstone** – Moonstone connects Aquarius with the powers of nature. It fosters patience and a greater sensitivity to one's environment. It also helps Aquarius tolerate the slower pace of others, who are hard-put to keep up with his restless search for new ideas.

◆ **Opal** – The water bearer's rich fantasy life is enhanced by opal, which also strengthens his creativity and helps him realize the ideas his fertile imagination produces.

◆ **Onyx** – Onyx reminds Aquarius that there is a world outside of his imagination that he can explore and experience. The calmness that onyx brings and its powerful vibrations can point to the path that the soul must travel.

◆ **Tourmaline** – Tourmaline is one of the most perfect stones on the planet. Its ability to reflect all the colors of light from the clearest white to the darkest black encourages Aquarius to avoid carelessness and superficiality and offers him steadfastness and peace.

Pisces (February 20 – March 20)

Pisces are extremely loveable people. They live in the world of feelings. Because they are so emotionally sensitive, they try to avoid embarrassment at all cost; they hide their vulnerability behind a wall of superficial self-confidence and brashness. Most, however, are not successful in maintaining this disguise. Those born under the sign of the fish don't like to be comforted; they shy away from being the center of attention. On the other hand, people often take advantage of their good nature and willingness to help others. They intuitively know that one can easily overcome rejection, defensiveness and resistance on the part of others by accepting them for what they are. They are often found engaged in the helping professions. If Pisces is endowed with self-awareness, remains true to his ideals and does not shut himself off from the world, he has the ability to penetrate the deepest mysteries and secrets of life. If, on the other hand, he feels helpless and

Pisces have the tendency to take on the problems and cares of others. They can easily be taken advantage of.

trapped within life's difficulties, he can easily give up and will do anything to avoid conflict.

The main gemstones for Pisces

◆ **Amethyst** – Amethyst will give Pisces the strength and courage to open his heart and mind to love. It furthers his creative gifts, helps him express his feelings and organize them in a coherent fashion.

◆ **Opal** – This stone is known for its fortunate properties. It brings with it harmony and happiness in life. These qualities can help spur the intuitive Piscean's meditations. It also can help restore cheerfulness to one stricken by depression or heartache.

◆ **Blue sapphire** – This gemstone helps those born under the sign of Pisces achieve higher levels of spirituality. Its deep blue color signifies divinity as well as loyalty, devotion and friendship. Sapphire also strengthens the critical faculty and promotes mental toughness.

◆ **Fluorite** – Fluorite enlarges understanding and can help Pisces grasp complex truths. When he comes to a dead end, it can restore his sense of proportion and give him an overview of the situation.

◆ **Sugilite** – Sugilite strengthens self-control. It prevents Pisceans from getting lost in daydreams. It protects them from being easily taken advantage of. It helps them to endure uncomfortable situations and gives them courage of their convictions and the ability to stand up for themselves in every situation.

Pisces are very sensitive. They can intuit other people's moods and vibrations.

Other important gemstones for Pisces

◆ **Garnet** – Garnet with its deep-red, fiery color endows Pisces with will power, physical energy, success and good luck. It helps him to stop daydreaming and to make his dreams a reality.

◆ **Agate** – Agate provides Pisces with stamina and patience. It helps him to keep his feet on the ground. Under its influence Pisces can gain self-confidence and make use of the positive sides of his personality.

◆ **Diamond** – No other sign is as strongly influenced by diamonds as the sensitive and emotional Pisces. Its clear vibration and pure, bright light combined with its concentrated hardness enable those born under the sign of the fish to recognize their sensitivities and susceptibilities.

◆ **Jade** - Jade supports and reinforces the loving and empathic nature of Pisces. It provides harmony and serenity and teaches trust in the wisdom of the heart. It opens the soul to the beauty and abundance of life.

◆ **Carnelian** – This gemstone helps Pisceans to put the past behind them and reconcile themselves to life. It provides these acutely sensitive people with a sense of stability but encourages them not to stagnate.

◆ **Rose quartz** – While providing inner harmony, rose quartz teaches this sign to better cope with the vicissitudes of life and the mood swings they can bring. Its radiance heals emotional wounds and awakens new life.

◆ **Citrine** – Citrine prevents Pisces from allowing his feelings to go unexpressed. Stifled emotion produces energy blockages in the solar plexus and leads to loss of peace of mind, dissatisfaction and irritability.

Aries (March 21 – April 20)

Aries wants to be the first and the best and for the most part succeeds in it. He never loses sight of his goals, neither in his personal or professional life. Aries keeps his youthful spirits well into old age. He often begins an entirely new life in retirement, but only after determining that it will be to his advantage. Those born under the sign of the ram are strong-willed people and do not like to relinquish control. That's why it's hard for them to give themselves to others; they are afraid of feeling weak and helpless. Sensing their own weaknesses makes them irritable and moody. They try to cover up their dissatisfaction. So one has to learn to forgive their moody outbursts. Aries has many good qualities. He does not rake up the past and exhibits stamina, graciousness, a sense of justice and openness. Because of his open nature Aries can easily go too far: he can laugh at what others find offensive. But if he senses that he has hurt someone's feelings, he is the first to apologize.

The main gemstones for Aries
◆ **Ruby** – Rubies can help Aries when he has lost sight of how to reach his goals. It fosters intuition and creativity. Rubies can increase his passion — especially towards his partner — which he

With great enthusiasm, Aries will achieve his realistic, attainable goals and can marshal tremendous resources to do so.

sometimes neglects, because he has so much internal resistance to letting go.

Aries is strong willed and self-confident. It is how he lives his life. He strives unwaveringly to reach his goals. He will easily surmount any obstacles in his path.

◆ **Garnet** – This gemstone increases self-confidence for Aries. It supports positive undertakings. It also prevents loss of perspective.

◆ **Carnelian** – Carnelian helps Aries, caught up in ambitious goals and schemes, not to forget the here and now. Aries likes to enjoy life. With the support of carnelian, he can allow himself the time needed for rest and recuperation.

◆ **Jasper** – Jasper symbolizes will power. It endows Aries with follow through and energy. Its red variant promotes sexual desire and fertility, but also inner peace and harmony. It strengthens the sense of self and its creative expression. Red jasper also tempers negative feelings such as anger, jealousy and hatred and is a good corrective for those easily distracted.

◆ **Kyanite** – This gemstone embodies heartsease and assists in meditation. It dissolves energy blockages and at the same time activates, calms and promotes the healthful flow of positive life energy. It drives out negative thoughts and produces cheerfulness. It promotes mental and spiritual growth in Aries. With its help Aries can ascend to higher planes.

Other important gemstones for Aries

◆ **Diamond** – Diamonds encourage those born under the sign of the ram to strive for higher goals. The diamond's clear light can also reveal their weaknesses and help in the struggle to overcome them.

◆ **Hematite** – This stone can bring Aries down to earth when he reaches too high and bring him into a better relationship with reality. It promotes purity and increases his level of physical energy.

◆ **Amethyst** – Amethyst can be a good complement to this sign's personality. Just as with the ruby, it helps Aries open up and guides him to inner spirituality. Armed with amethyst and his own will power, he can do something entirely unexpected, surprising those who see him as a single-minded realist.

Taurus (April 21 – May 20)

A happy family, peaceful surroundings, these are the most important things for those born in Taurus. Taurus will think carefully before acting. He has no interest in making quick or impulsive decisions but knows that everything in nature takes time to reach fulfillment. So he will give himself the time and leisure to allow his thoughts to find their proper form. But once he enters upon a course of action, he will persevere until the goal is reached. Those born in Taurus are dubious about change and innovation, and material security is always very important to them. And to avoid ever finding themselves in need, they will stretch each penny as far as it will go. For this reason they are sometimes seen as tight-fisted and penny-pinching. But that is not really the case. Taurus is a true friend and will go to great lengths to help someone in need. But only when it is really necessary. This sign does not crave the limelight. Taurus is happiest sitting in the second row. Good at problem solving, he will take his time and come up with practical solutions. He is naturally skilled at working with his hands.

The main gemstones for Taurus

◆ **Rhodochrosite** – This gemstone has a particularly salutary effect on Taurus. It promotes a positive self-image and the spontaneous expression of emotion. Taurus often neglects these aspects of himself, especially when he is worried about his financial future. This can transform his natural frugality into miserliness. But rhodochrosite will combat this tendency.

◆ **Rose quartz** – Rose quartz provides the underpinning for those born under the sign of the bull to love and care for themselves. When faced with professional or personal difficulties, they can find in rose quartz peace and ease of mind. This frees them for clear thinking and fresh undertakings.

Taurus individuals are family-oriented. They will do anything, even work themselves to the bone, for the ones they love.

◆ **Agate** – For those born under the sign of Taurus, agate strengthens their thoughtful, down-to-earth characters. Agate's sheltering influence allows them to make their dreams a reality. It also helps them to live within their means.

◆ **Chrysocolla** – This gemstone opens the eyes of Taurus to the beauties of nature and helps him to see the oneness of heaven and earth. Then he can free himself from doubt and make his life richer and happier. Stress and anxiety will also be reduced.

◆ **Aventurine** – Aventurine brings patience and tranquility. It encourages Taurus to dream. This can be extremely beneficial for those bogged down in a world of materiality.

◆ **Zircon** – Zircon leads to an awareness of impermanence. It helps Taurus find his way in times of loss, sorrow and death. It counteracts the narrowing of one's vision, bringing reconciliation with reality while stimulating the powers of imagination. The brighter varieties are particularly lucky for Taurus.

Other important gemstones for Taurus

◆ **Diamond** – This precious stone give Taurus the insight to recognize higher values and ideals and not think only of personal gain.

◆ **Malachite** – Malachite lightens life's burdens for Taurus and helps him through times of change. It teaches that everything in the universe is in the process of change. And that man as an integral part of the cosmos must also undergo transformation and renewal.

◆ **Emerald** – Emerald imbues the oft-burdened Taurus with the energy and freshness of youth. It provides insight and speeds thought processes while enhancing concentration.

◆ **Obsidian** – Obsidian helps Taurus connect with his feelings and stay grounded. This allows him to weather the storms that life can bring.

◆ **Citrine** – Citrine provides Taurus with the sense of safety and security that is so important to him. Taurus loves to eat. Citrine helps in detoxification and promotes healthier skin.

Gemini (May 21 – June 21)

Geminis are sociable. They easily make new friends and don't have a problem discussing the intimate details of their life with new-found acquaintances.

Geminis love new things, are deeply curious and will readily listen to others. They want to learn, sample and experience all that the world has to offer. They are interested in everything. They find it hard to imagine that someone is uninterested in the problems and difficulties that others face. Their most impressive gift is a striking linguistic ability. They can clearly express in words things that others can barely conceive of. They have a need to find a verbal equivalence for all of their experiences and impressions. Through their highly developed intellectual capacity, they have the ability to see all sides of a question. They rebel against narrow patterns of thought. This inner flexibility and freedom can also lead to ambivalence. Even when Gemini has concluded that a course of action is reasonable and profitable, he can change direction on the spur of the moment. Gemini will find success in any profession that calls for creativity, flexibility, openness and communication skills. There the many-sided Gemini will be in his element. Older Geminis are very gifted in dealing with young people.

The main gemstones for Gemini
- **Amber** – Amber gives Gemini peace in his search for new and undiscovered territories. In its warm glow he will find the needed confidence to realize his plans.
- **Citrine** – Citrine lights Gemini's path, thereby providing the emotional clarity he needs to find his way through difficulties. It also helps him ground spiritual insights in the real world and expand his emotional life.
- **Carnelian** – This is a particularly potent gemstone for Gemini. It supports spiritual vitality. And through its connection with the earth, it helps keep the volatile Gemini on course. It serves as a firm platform from which he can embark on his spiritual quest without the danger of getting lost in a maze.
- **Yellow sapphire** – Yellow sapphire lends support to all of Gemini's plans and goals. It strengthens his will and critical faculties. It helps him be more decisive and feel comfortable with his decisions. Sapphire has particularly effective healing power in cases of stress, anxiety and nervous disorders.
- **Celestite** – This stone has become rather hard to find. Its clear white and light blue varieties confer relaxation and calmness of mind. Its has a soothing effect and endows its possessor with a clear and awakened spirit. It is also very helpful in combating the feeling of being overwhelmed. With its help Gemini can enjoy all of his various interests and manage his busy schedule and still preserve his good spirits and diplomatic talents.
- **Apophylite** – Apophylite alleviates nervousness and helps Gemini find peace of mind even in the most difficult situation. Just as it can be used in cases of bodily paralysis, so it can ensure that its possessor will never become paralyzed by anxiety.

Other important gemstones for Gemini
- **Aquamarine** – Aquamarine helps Gemini attain unity with the deepest levels of his being. It can show the open-minded and susceptible Gemini that true freedom requires certain boundaries.

Geminis are charming, knowledgeable, quick and imaginative. Their restless curiosity leads them to always seek out new sensations.

With the support of aquamarine the Gemini can overcome resistances and limitations to his spiritual freedom.

◆ **Rock crystal** – Rock crystal provides Gemini with inner clarity and paves the way for spiritual exploration and meditation.

◆ **Chalcedony** – The blue-white variety of chalcedony will bring Gemini inner peace. It helps him listen to his inner voice and be sensitive to the beauty of color. It makes his speech calmer and even more precise. In addition, it can help him avoid pitfalls along the spiritual path.

◆ **Moss agate** – Moss agate offers Geminis insight and understanding of different cultures and lifestyles. It gives them the ability to understand the common lot of humanity and live in fellowship with other people.

◆ **Tiger's eye** – This gem encourages Gemini to direct the gaze within and supports clear thinking.

◆ **Turquoise** – Turquoise protects Gemini from negative influences that can easily disturb his aura. It absorbs unhealthy vibrations and allows him to maintain his spiritual purity and vitality.

Cancer (June 22 – July 22)

Cancer has a gentle soul. He can give himself others and cares for all growing things. The protection of the family circle is very important for Cancer.

Cancers need to feel secure. They keep their financial affairs to themselves. They map out their future in the smallest detail. They choose their partners with the utmost care and can spend a long time looking for the right one. But once they have found the right person, they look no farther. Most celebrate golden wedding anniversaries. Cancers change careers reluctantly, only when it's clear that their current employment offers no prospects for advancement. They are guided by their feelings. Once they allow someone into their inmost circle, they will remain true to that person without reservation. It is, however, difficult for them to share their sorrows and anxieties with others. They keep their feelings bottled up and for that reason are prone to stomach and intestinal maladies. They can get so caught up in their private grief that they take refuge in a world of fantasy and daydream. They need praise and encouragement, or they can feel blocked. But surprisingly Cancers can also display considerable ambition. This can help them overcome the low self-esteem that stems from living in a world that values only money and position.

The main gemstones for Cancer

◆ **Emerald** – Emerald provides Cancer with stability and alleviates mood swings. Its deep green reflects life's meaningfulness. It absorbs negative vibrations and protects against them.

◆ **Moonstone** – This gemstone teaches Cancers that one makes progress only by striving for the highest ideals. It forces them to stop daydreaming and to face reality.

◆ **Aventurine** – Aventurine can bring Cancers peace in heart and mind. When caught in the turbulence of their powerful emotions, they can find solace and calm in green aventurine.

◆ **Chalcedony** – The milky white, silver variety is the best for Cancers. It is especially helpful when they feel like retreating into their shell and can't find a way to share their feelings with others. It also helps them fight off negative influences, so that when it feels like the world is closing in on them, they can regain their creativity and break free of the bonds that imprison them.

◆ **Jade** – Jade gives Cancers the confidence to trust in their feelings. A bit of jade kept in the pocket as a touchstone will provide a sense of security in difficult situations.

◆ **Opal** – Opal impresses upon Cancer that he is entitled to his own feelings. This allows him to find a way through difficulties. It supports his striving for harmony.

◆ **Pearl** – Because of their luster and smoothness, pearls are natural symbols of beauty and perfection. They confer wisdom and sincerity on Cancer, helping to guard against danger. They also provide contentment in old age and moderate mood swings.

◆ **Olivine** – The Cancer who is beset by the anxiety and depression that come from holding too much inside should turn to olivine. It is also effective in treating skin disease and metabolic disorders.

◆ **Chrysoprase** – Chrysoprase has a calming effect on Cancers. It helps them reach a balance between the conscious and unconscious spheres. It encourages them to strive for harmony and deepens their ability to connect with others.

◆ **Chrysocolla** – This gemstone gives Cancer serenity and tolerance and stimulates both intuition and imagination. It is an antidote against the poison of hate and anger; it helps its

Cancer can be easily wounded. If attacked, he retreats into his shell, rather than stand his ground.

possessor see that the world is a beautiful place. Its benign influence will enrich the lives of those born under the sign of the crab.

Other important stones for Cancer

◆ **Carnelian** – Carnelian channels the earth's magnetism. It can aid Cancer, who feels abandonment and loss particularly keenly. It teaches him that nature is constantly changing and that nothing in the universe can stand still.

◆ **Rhodochrosite** – Its combination of pink and orange lends new strength to Cancer's self-awareness. It opens his eyes to unimagined possibilities. Ordinarily, Cancer would dismiss these as untenable. But this attitude can lead to the dimming of one's spiritual light. Rhodochrosite prevents that from happening.

◆ **Sodalite** – Sodalite strengthens one's mental faculties. Its blue color helps Cancer keep a cool head in the midst of powerful emotions. It also encourages him to return to face the challenges from which he has retreated.

Leo loves to be the center of attention. His positive, magnetic personality influences those around him.

Leo (July 23 – August 23)

Leos like to be the center of attention. They are charming and bask in the admiration of others The sign of Leo corresponds to the sun, as does Leo's character. Leos enjoy discussion and don't shy away from arguments. Self-assured and full of vitality, they radiate optimism and energy. But they find some things hard to take, especially rules and regulations that hamper their creativity. Leos are usually found in upper management; they are fair to their employees. They ask a lot out of them, but their demands are always reasonable.

The Leo who has not learned to recognize his purpose in life can become overly dependent upon the admiration and validation he gets from other people. He can lose sight of compassion and understanding, particularly towards those he sees as standing in his way. Leo burns up so much physical and mental energy that he runs the risk of depleting himself. He suffers deeply and wants to be comforted and taken care of. Then he can return to claim his place in the spotlight. Leo's natural charm and intelligence help him to quickly recognize his shortcomings, take pains to nourish the healthy aspects of his character and combat negative influences.

The main gemstones for Leo

◆ **Rock crystal** – Rock crystal imbues Leo with strength and inner composure and intensifies positive vibrations. In times of adversity, rock crystal can help him regain his natural confidence and optimism.

◆ **Larimar** – This gemstone aids Leo in resolving old problems and leads to new ways of thinking and dealing with situations. It protects him from exhaustion and the negative energy that can cast a shadow over his sunny disposition.

◆ **Diamond** – Diamonds are the gemstones with the clearest light. The diamond's piercing rays remind Leo that true leadership – whether in personal or professional endeavors – involves service.

◆ **Chrysoberyl** – Chrysoberyl is highly beneficial for Leos. It leads to improved relationships with partners and subordinates. It brings tolerance and harmony and fosters gentleness in personal dealings. It helps Leos recover their optimism during trying times.

◆ **Topaz** – Pink topaz is the lucky stone for Leos. It fosters honesty, sincerity and fairness in the drive for business and personal success. It also gives Leos the necessary distance to think things over, so that they don't become frazzled and lose their sense of proportion.

Diamonds motivate Leos. Under their influence, they can reach peak physical condition.

Other important stones for Leo

◆ **Onyx** – To benefit Leos, to make their high-flying plans come true, onyx must be pure black. This stone keeps their minds free and flexible.

◆ **Yellow-gold citrine** – Citrine in this color brings Leo relaxation and rest, when he becomes drained by his strenuous efforts to reach his goals. It awakens compassion and the necessary understanding to consider the feelings of others, as he strives for plaudits and success.

◆ **Garnet** – Garnet strengthens Leo's will power and endurance. It balances his sexual energy so that he can experience the deepest joys of love. Its positive influence will also make itself felt in his working life.

◆ **Peridot** – Peridot displays one of the most beautiful and clear shades of green. It keeps Leo young, strengthens the immune system and revivifies the aura.

◆ **Selenite** – With its pearly luster, this stone provides Leo with the modesty and self-control that will best set off his loving and attractive nature.

◆ **Tiger's eye** – Tiger's eye reinforces Leo's mental powers and helps him become more inward-looking. Thus he can come to grips with his weaknesses and overcome limitations. Then he will discover that well-being and happiness depend more upon one's spiritual development than on outward measures of success.

◆ **Tourmaline** – This gemstone has an especially powerful influence. Its parallel structure directs light rays and transforms them into positive energy. That is why tourmaline is of immediate benefit for the psychosomatic ailments to which Leos are particularly susceptible.

Virgo (August 24 – September 23)

Virgos need to feel they are in control. This can lead to a loss of spontaneity and exaggerated deference to rules and regulations.

Virgos are true friends. They carefully consider what is best for themselves and their families. Spontaneity has little appeal for them. They love system and order above all things. Because of this they tend to plan for every eventuality, even in love and romance. Their love of order can lead them to be overly fastidious. They are unfailingly punctual and expect the same from others. They will not betray their highly developed sense of duty and responsibility even if it causes them pain and suffering. They have a tendency to dismiss as unimportant, things they don't fully understand and sometimes can be a bit snobbish. This can create obstacles to their spiritual development.

Virgos are not easy to get to know, but if you win one over, you have gained a real treasure. Virgos are not fair-weather friends. They will stick by you through thick and thin.

The main gemstones for Virgo

◆ **Tiger's eye** – Tiger's eye leads Virgo away from overly structured activities and lightens the burdens of daily life. It lessens his need for security and stops his second-guessing himself in order to conform to other people's expectations. It also helps him to be less of a perfectionist, makes him more aware of his feelings and motivates him to open himself up without fear.

◆ **Gold topaz** – This has always been regarded as a stone of wisdom and protection. It gives Virgos the courage and perseverance to implement their life plans. It ensures that they work honestly and fairly at achieving them. Gold topaz is also the gemstone of self-realization.

◆ **Jasper** – Jasper fosters modesty and self-restraint, strengthening one's sense of reality and connection to the earth. Yellow jasper provides mental acuity, red jasper inner harmony. It gives Virgo physical and psychological strength.

◆ **Citrine** – This is the stone of self-confidence and individuality. It has always been considered talismanic and is particularly lucky for those who have a distinct goal in life or ambitious plans and need time and energy to fulfill them. Thus it is particularly compatible with Virgo's character. In times of confusion and frustration, it provides good cheer.

◆ **Carnelian** – Carnelian promotes idealism and the awareness of social issues. It supports Virgos in their aspirations to help others and gives them the strength to do so. Red carnelian symbolizes activity and promotes energy. All forms of carnelian help Virgos take pleasure in living, which they tend to lose sight of. It reinforces their naturally steadfast characters and gives them the boost needed to undertake new enterprises.

◆ **Ametrine** – This multi-colored stone consists of citrine and amethyst. It helps Virgo gain maturity and find a way of life that suits him. It also allows him to express his feelings. It dissolves emotional blocks and attacks the stagnation that hampers the growth of creativity and spirituality.

Other important stones for Virgo

◆ **Azurite** – The pure light of azurite confers wisdom and truth on the soul. It helps Virgo forego an exaggerated need for order and enhances the romantic and spiritual sides of his nature.

Virgos are good at detailed work. They like things to be orderly. If they can avoid overdoing this tendency, they can be of great service to those around them.

◆ **Hematite** – With the help of hematite Virgo will be able to withstand hard times, great loss, career disappointments and manage extreme stress. Its metallic silver luster nourishes body and soul in times of adversity.

◆ **Jade** – Jade provides Virgo with health and vitality. Its deep green color intensifies the flow of energy between chakras and loosens blockages of bodily fluids. This strengthens the immune system and allows confused emotions to become disentangled.

◆ **Lapis lazuli** – Lapis keeps Virgo from being too modest and self-controlled. It is a stone of power and nobility and can heal body, mind and spirit. It directs Virgo's gaze within to the source of all strength and healing.

◆ **Opal** – Opal helps Virgos appreciate the rich variety of life and open their awareness to spheres of action that seemed closed to them. In this way they can become more spontaneous.

◆ **Ruby** – When Virgo feels that he lacks the strength to go on, ruby allows energy to bubble up from its deepest source. Its deep red radiance stimulates the chakras.

◆ **Sodalite** – Sodalite possesses intense power. Its deep blue color represents spiritual strength. It serves to connect the material and spiritual worlds. It will increase Virgo's inner awareness and help it find expression in daily life.

Libra (September 24 – October 23)

Libra is always looking for the ideal relationship, dreaming of a perfectly harmonious partnership with another person.

Libras are masters of the art of living. They seek balance in all things. Very individualistic, they actively strive for justice, beauty and harmony. They do not like to make decisions, but they have an intuitive sense of where they are going and how to get there. Consequently, they avoid many pitfalls; it is as if they were being guided by an unseen hand. Their first instincts are usually right. Libras cannot bear to live in a conflict-ridden atmosphere and are sometimes quick to compromise. They are willing to suffer disadvantages in order to keep the peace. Their desire for harmony can therefore be detrimental to some Libras, who end up sacrificing their own interests to please others. They need to be on their guard against this tendency.

When Libras learn to justly appreciate their inner happiness, they can shake off the fear they have of losing, even if only for a short time, the affection of others, be it in their personal or professional life.

The main gemstones for Libra

◆ **Smoky quartz** – Smoky quartz is a protective stone for the Libra who seeks to make his life pleasant and free from turmoil. It provides the concentration needed to resolve problems and challenges. Smoky quartz can bring new ideas to Libra and help him maintain balance and a positive self-image. Anxiety, neurosis and depression will recede into the background and new beginnings come more easily.

◆ **Jade** – Jade offers Libra vitality and health. Its deep green color intensifies the flow of energy between the chakras and dissolves blockages of bodily fluids. It strengthens the immune system and allows Libra to put his thoughts and feelings in order. From inner harmony the Libra finds his way to the outside world.

◆ **Aquamarine** – A most important ally for Libra. Its vibrations bring inner freedom and mental and spiritual clarity. Thus Libra can stand up for his own ideas and desires, and not give in so easily to the wishes of others.

◆ **Sugilite** – Sugilite encourages freedom, self-definition and self-restraint. It helps Libras advance from subordinate positions. Under its benign influence, Libra can come to better terms with himself and enjoy spending time alone.

◆ **Star Sapphire** – This beautiful stone supports positive plans and goals. It clarifies the will, sharpens the critical faculty and creates a sense of peace. With star sapphire, Libras can make decisions without second-guessing themselves.

◆ **Chrysocolla** – This stone fosters tolerance and harmony. It calms the stressed-out Libra and helps him let go of anger and hatred more quickly. When his inner balance is upset by excessive emotion, chrysocolla will show Libra the way back to his natural inner composure.

◆ **Tourmaline** – Blue tourmaline emits a message of peace. It keeps mind and soul in balance and allows Libra to live in harmony under difficult conditions. It encourages him to look within to find his true being and more easily recognize his destiny. Blue tourmaline helps its possessor take responsibility for his own life.

Libras possess the enviable quality of maintaining their optimism in the most difficult circumstances.

Other important stones for Libra

Libras know that they need to keep their self-esteem high, otherwise the positive flow of energy will be blocked.

◆ **Malachite** – Malachite embodies the deep healing green of nature. It reflects the beauty of the natural world as it transforms itself through the course of the seasons. Nature's innate harmony, its ecological balance of plant and animal life, speaks deeply to this sign. Malachite cheers Libra and lifts his spirits in times of trouble.

◆ **Turquoise** – Turquoise brings together within itself the blue vibration of the heavens and the green of the earth. This is an ideal combination for Libra, who is always looking for harmony and balance. Since turquoise captures the uplifting vibrations of the cosmos, it is an invaluable ally for those facing adversity.

◆ **Diamond** – Diamond's crystal purity strengthens those born under the sign of Libra and reveals things that have been hidden. It teaches them to recognize the need for inner harmony and the beauty of the true self. With the insight conferred by diamonds, Libras learn to recognize the multifarious variety in humans and the natural world that surrounds them and attune themselves to cosmic forces.

◆ **Carnelian** – Carnelian increases vitality and acuity. It lengthens the attention span and helps Libra concentrate on the task at hand and be more productive.

◆ **Kunzite** – Kunzite brings inner peace and security to Libra. It gives him the confidence to make the necessary decisions. It makes Libra strong and self-reliant.

◆ **Obsidian** – Obsidian opens Libra's mind to unfulfilled dreams and desires. This stone, which comes from deep within the earth's core, has the capacity to reveal all that has been hidden. When Libra recognizes the source of his discontent, he can address the problem and overcome physical and psychic impediments.

Scorpio (October 24 – November 22)

Scorpio endures to the bitter end. He is honest and never forgets. When he wants something, he will not rest until he has experienced it. And once having begun a course of action, he will do whatever it takes to arrive at his goal.

Scorpio does not tolerate criticism. And with his elephant's memory, he won't ever forget uncalled-for slights. He is justly proud of his immense will power, which can overcome all obstacles. Even if he cannot achieve his goal right away, he knows he will get there in time. And he usually succeeds, thanks to his incredible endurance and ability to focus. But his focus on an objective can lead him into difficult situations. If he finds himself up against a brick wall, he can fall into a deep depression. Then he tries to break through his own boundaries. If he drops his guard with someone and is not taken advantage of, he can become a true friend and partner to that person. Scorpios like to live well. They enjoy socializing and appreciate fine restaurants. But they are connoisseurs, only the finest food and wine meet their exacting standards. They do not compromise; they will agree only with the truth. Speaking the truth can make one lonely, especially when done so without regard to the feelings of others. But that is the price one pays for being a Scorpio.

Scorpio has a high opinion of himself. His self-confidence is not easily shaken. He has to look very closely at himself to admit his own mistakes.

The main gemstones for Scorpio

◆ **Hematite** – Hematite is an especially helpful stone for one born under the sign of Scorpio. It offers him patience and peace of mind. With its wonderful earth tones, it enables him to compromise and be more trusting of his partner, to put aside his own wishes and give himself to another.

◆ **Coral** – Red coral helps Scorpio fully enjoy life. It brings joy, energy and sensuality and protects him from envy and resentment. It helps him deal with jealousy and self-doubt.

◆ **Fluorite** – Fluorite promotes intellectual development. It harmonizes the positive and negative aspects of the intellect. Fluorite helps Scorpios to use their intellectual gifts, endurance and will power for the good of others and saves them from overweening egotism.

◆ **Obsidian** – Obsidian loosens rigidities. Obsidian not only eases psychological problems, it also relaxes constrictions in the shoulder and neck areas that often plague Scorpio. This comes from his iron will, which does not allow him to let go and give his thoughts free rein.

◆ **Sard** – Sard is the gemstone of justice. It encourages Scorpio's sense of justice, while keeping fanaticism in check. Sard sharpens the mind, promotes openness in dealings with other people, solidifies friendships and relationships. It guides the egocentric and introverted individual to become more outgoing toward those close to him.

◆ **Spinel** – Red spinel promotes determination. It helps Scorpio recognize worthwhile goals and gives him the energy to reach them. It lessens fears, especially of major changes in employment or divorce, which can discourage even the hardy Scorpio. Spinel strengthens the soul's healing power.

◆ **Tourmaline** – Red tourmaline helps Scorpio relinquish plans and ideas that his extraordinary will power cannot bring to fulfillment. With its assistance Scorpio can let go without falling into depression or losing his self-esteem. With red tourmaline he can approach others with greater awareness and respect for their wishes and ideas.

Shortcomings like overweening ambition or the refusal to accept criticism can be corrected through the use of healing stones.

◆ **Garnet** – Garnet allows Scorpio to transform his emotional strength and sexual desire into true love. Its red rays bring him into harmony with the heart of the beloved.

Other important stones for Scorpio

◆ **Agate** – Agate's crystalline inclusions give Scorpio the purity and clarity to recognize his inner nature. With its help, he can maintain this inner purity and face any difficulty that life has to offer.

◆ **Chalcedony** – Chalcedony supports Scorpio in difficult times. In his darkest hour when everything seems lost, chalcedony can restore self-esteem and trust in his own abilities and creativity. Having regained his self-confidence, he can return to the fray with new energy and succeed in all of his plans.

◆ **Jade** – Jade gives Scorpio confidence and *joie de vivre*. It enables him to acknowledge the beauty in the world and accept it without compromise. This will help him to become more sensitive and sympathetic and enjoy life more. His happiness will spread to those around him.

◆ **Malachite** – This gemstone gives Scorpio the ability to acknowledge his shortcomings and better deal with them. It increases his compassion for himself and others. It helps him to speak hard truths in a more tactful and gentle way.

♦ **Ruby** – With rubies Scorpios can transform their emotions and sexual desires into true, lasting love. Their red glow ensures harmony in love relations. They teach constancy and point the way to perfect oneness with the cosmos.

Sagittarius (November 23 – December 21)

Sagittarians are usually in good spirits and want to share their sunny outlook with others. They have a knack for being happy. Their positive energy and their sensitivity to the beauties in nature and in other people make it certain that they are well liked and sought after. With their innate cheerfulness and social skills they are wonderfully gifted at passing along what they know to others. Consequently, one can often find Sagittarians working as ministers, counselors and teachers. They are also well-suited for journalism.

Sagittarius knows that life offers prospects of endless beauty. He wants to visit foreign lands and embark on life's grand adventure.

Along with their good nature, Sagittarians are endowed with a sense of responsibility. Because they possess such a clear sense of right and wrong, they find it hard to witness injustice. This can lead them to lose their composure, and impatience can flare up into anger. But the storm clouds soon blow themselves away. Fortunately, Sagittarians are constitutionally incapable of bearing grudges. They are always on the look out for new sensations, which can threaten their stability. Then the only constant in their life is constant change. Because they are so certain their own view of things is the right one, they sometimes find it difficult to appreciate that others may have a different point of view.

The main gemstones for Sagittarius
♦ **Lapis lazuli** – Lapis enables Sagittarius to realize his aspirations and share his plans with others. It also helps him find a partner with whom he can share his love and who will accompany him on life's adventure.
♦ **Obsidian** – Obsidian will help Sagittarius in pursuing his goals and in his journey of self-discovery. It protects him from doubts and negative influences that could constrict his talents. Obsidian can help Sagittarius overcome emotional blockages and unhealthy vibrations and restore his natural optimism.

Sagittarius is open and cheerful, and is generally well liked. But he has to guard against pride and arrogance.

◆ **Aventurine** – Aventurine enhances all of the positive qualities of one born under the sign of the archer. Its connection to the earth's magnetic field strengthens his inner cheerfulness and the positive vibrations that flow from him. As a result, he can make a positive impact on the world around him. Recognition of this fact will make him even stronger and more self-confident.

◆ **Herkimer diamond** – Herkimer diamond promotes clear thinking and self-esteem. It stands for openness and the free expression of ideas. It gives Sagittarius strength for new adventures. To get the best effect one should concentrate on the stone and project the awareness of the desired result onto it. After using the stone, discharging it under running water will neutralize it, so that it can be used again.

◆ **Sodalite** – This stone gives Sagittarius the strength to defend his point of view and remain true to himself. It widens his powers, helps him concentrate on essential matters and guides him to higher levels of understanding.

◆ **Dumortierite** – Dumortierite helps Sagittarius relate to others with tolerance. It reinforces his innate positive qualities, enriching the intuition. With its help Sagittarius can quickly recognize his limitations and learn how to rise above them. The deep blue variety increases patience and consideration for others, qualities that Sagittarius needs in his everyday dealings. It is the gemstone of loving acceptance.

◆ **Apatite** – The spiritual power of apatite endows Sagittarius with openness and joy in relating to others. It is very helpful in combating lack of motivation and irritability. When anger seems to gain the upper hand, apatite can keep it in check. It is also a powerful antidote to grief and negative emotions. It helps Sagittarius regain his good nature and equilibrium and releases inhibitions.

◆ **Chalcedony** – Chalcedony directs Sagittarius to look inward toward essentials and protects him from restlessness and makes him more reliable.

◆ **Spinel** – The deep blue variety of spinel fosters perseverance and endurance in times of crisis. Especially those Sagittarians who become easily distracted will find this stone very helpful.

◆ **Zircon** – Blue zircon helps Sagittarius rebound from loss. It promotes clear understanding and remedies mental imbalances. It encourages Sagittarius to acknowledge reality but also promotes dreaming. This gemstone will help him process the new impressions garnered from travel and social intercourse, while avoiding overstimulation.

Other important stones for Sagittarius

♦ **Topaz** – The almost transparent blue topaz is a true companion for Sagittarius on all his travels. It will help him find his way through the wilderness and give him the strength and courage to carry on.

♦ **Moonstone** – Moonstone will awaken new depths of creativity and imagination in Sagittarius. Its significant powers stem from its deep connection to the earth. It will give Sagittarius greater endurance and protect him from impulsiveness and self-doubt. Moonstone promotes even-temperedness and inner peace.

♦ **Amethyst** – Amethyst encourages Sagittarius to trust his instincts. When he has been knocked down and begins to doubt his core values, amethyst will give him the spiritual power to recognize life's meaningfulness. Then he will be able to once again listen to his inner voice calling him to a higher purpose.

♦ **Opal** – This gemstone is a lucky charm for Sagittarius. Its many colors mirror the endless variety of life. Sagittarius is naturally receptive to the wondrous riches and changing colors of the world around him. Opal guides him to a deeper understanding of the many facets of the spiritual realm.

♦ **Rose quartz** – With rose quartz Sagittarius will find the tenderness and love his mercurial personality sometimes lacks. Under its influence Sagittarius will feel more secure and content, especially when faced with the anxieties that accompany charting a new course.

♦ **Tourmaline** – Tourmaline helps Sagittarius better direct his energies and talents. It provides him with the material support to embark on new undertakings. But it also reminds him that inner well-being is the true source of happiness. Sagittarius needs to work on his own development to maintain his good spirits: money, status or social acceptance are not the only things that count.

Sagittarius can run the danger of giving too much weight to the high opinion in which others hold him. He can end up thinking he is never wrong.

The Energy Fields
of Crystals and
Gemstones

Healing stones transmit their power through color and vibration. Experience their healing force in the body and learn to recognize the effect of gems and colors on the chakras, the body's energy centers.

Energy and Color

Almost anyone can appreciate the color of healing stones, but to experience the power of their vibrations, one has to actually make use of them. We can consider all physical, intellectual and psychic processes, all sensation, thought and feeling, as chemical reactions within the body. These consume and create energy. Sometimes there can be too much energy in the body and at other times too little. Many colors emit positive energy; others have an equalizing effect. By properly using color, one can regulate the body's energy level, making up for deficits or siphoning off excesses. That is why certain colors appeal to people in certain situations. The colors of healing stones work on the human organism and psyche. The intense play of light of gemstones can have a calming or stimulating effect; it can purify or heal.

Meditations on gemstones can lead to physical health, psychological balance, self-discovery and inner clarity.

The frequencies of light that stones emit are particularly important. They have a direct influence on the body's biochemical processes. In addition, stones reflect the body's chemistry. Stones consist of crystals whose smallest singular component is the atom. These are in constant motion. But because the vibrations of energy are not visible, stones seem to be solid objects. Their energy can be positive, negative or neutral, but only by its effects can this be known. Just as one feels more or less comfortable in certain environments, so one can feel positive or negative vibrations from contact with certain stones.

The Effects of Color

The Indian Ayurvedic tradition teaches us that the health of the body and mind is dependent upon a number of factors: our thoughts, dreams and attitude towards work, our environment, neighbors, pleasant and unpleasant sounds, smells and colors as well as the influence of gemstones and crystals. In this holistic conception of the human person, color plays a particularly important role. All of the colors of the spectrum that we see in the world around us find a perfect correspondence in the microcosm within each of us. In ancient cultures, people would paint themselves with bright colors to connect with the mysterious strength of the soul. They understood that each color has a deep inner meaning. This still holds true today, even though much of the ancient knowledge concerning these matters has been lost. Color has a healing effect not only upon the soul but upon the totality of the human organism. To fully grasp the healing power of color one must study the different colors and their properties.

Colors, Their Meaning and Therapeutic Use

Color	Meaning	Therapeutic Use
Red	Activity, energy, stamina, joy in living, sexuality, love	Supports circulatory and metabolic systems. Strengthens will power and keeps one active
Orange	Vitality, ambition, fertility, erotic feelings	Adds balance and calmness; promotes the flow of energy
Yellow	Optimism, cheerfulness, success, generosity, satisfaction, élan vital	Stimulates all organs, increases energy levels, strengthens the immune system; removes inhibitions and fear of relationships
Green	Warmheartedness, friendship, openness, freedom, harmony, peace, empathy, self-renewal	Harmonizes, detoxifies and regenerates; enhances emotion, leads one to inner peace and strengthens the will to live
Blue	Faithfulness, loyalty, openness, freedom (light blue); responsibility and respect for others (dark blue)	Calms, activates the digestive system and circulation of fluids in the body; relaxes and combats anxiety and discouragement
Violet	Insight, spirituality, transformation, determination, peace and devotion to others.	Regulates respiration and strengthens digestion; inspires, helps with grief and promotes serenity
Black	Detachment, seclusion, ignorance, pride, elegance, security	Dissolves energy blockages and tension, relieves pain; offers protection for the self
White	Purity, sincerity, clarity, innocence, truth, perfection, immortality	Helps with all deficiencies and weaknesses, provides energy and leads to self-realization

Gemstones and the Chakras

The practice of acupuncture and reflexology has confirmed that the smallest regions of the body can have a significant influence on an entire organ. The same principle underpins the practice of healing with stones. Healing stones are particularly powerful when used in conjunction with the body's energy centers, the chakras.

Indian doctors and therapists have posited that sickness is always linked to a disturbance in the flow of energy within the body. The free flow of this energy provides cells and organs with what they need to sustain their healthy functioning. In fact, health can be defined as the state in which energy is flowing unimpeded through the chakras. But when for whatever reason the flow of energy is blocked, a part of the body will not function properly. These blockages can arise from physical complaints or psychic conflicts. There are seven primary chakras in the human body vibrating at seven different frequencies, each sharing information with the others. In addition, there are secondary chakras in the hands and feet.

If you want to use stones to influence the chakras, you should find a smooth flat stone, whose color matches the chakra you want to affect. Lay it directly on that chakra for one hour a day. It is very important to be quiet and rest during this process. You can also tape the stone directly on the chakra overnight.

Each chakra has a special duty and vibrates at a particular frequency. This corresponds to the vibrations of certain colors and minerals.

First chakra – Root chakra

The root chakra lies between the rectum and the genital area. It absorbs energy from the earth. It is the energy center for all of the body's hard tissue: bone, spinal column, teeth and nails. It influences the intestines and prostate, as well as blood and cell formation.

◆ **Energy of the first chakra** – A disturbance in the root chakra leads to addiction, uncontrolled or diminished sexuality, digestive disorders and obesity. If energy flows smoothly through this chakra, one will feel a deep connection to nature.

◆ **Stones for the chakra** – Stones recommended for treating the root chakra are garnet, hematite, red jasper, coral, onyx, rhodonite, ruby and black tourmaline.

◆ **Color for the chakra** – Red. In all cultures red is the color of life, warmth and vitality. Red stimulates the life force.

Symbol for the first chakra, the root chakra

Symbol for the second chakra, the sacral chakra

Second Chakra – Sacral chakra

The sacral chakra lies above the pubic bone and opens frontward. This center governs the flow of all of the body's liquid elements: blood, lymph, sweat, digestive juices, sperm and urine, as well as tears.

◆ **Energy of the second chakra** – A disturbance in the second chakra causes sexual problems. Life may seem to lose its meaning. When the balance of energy is restored, one becomes more open and is able to enjoy life.

◆ **Stones for the chakra** – Stones recommended for treating the sacral chakra are orange beryl, orange jasper, carnelian and citrine.

◆ **Color for the chakra** – Orange. Orange is the symbolic color of the sacral chakra. It is warm and positive. It is the color of nourishment and circulation.

Symbol for the third chakra, the navel chakra

Third Chakra – Navel or Solar Plexus Chakra

The third chakra, the solar plexus, lies above the navel. This chakra governs the stomach, liver, spleen and gall bladder, the digestive system and the autonomic nervous system.

◆ **Energy of the navel chakra** – When energy flows uninterruptedly through the third chakra, one feels a deep sense of inner peace. Blockages will create discontent, restlessness and discouragement.

◆ **Stones for the chakra** – Stones recommended for treating the navel chakra are tiger's eye, topaz, yellow tourmaline and citrine.

◆ **Color for the chakra** – Yellow. Yellow corresponds to the third chakra. It stands for intelligence.

Symbol for the fourth chakra, the heart chakra

Fourth chakra – Heart Chakra

The heart chakra lies in the middle of the chest and opens frontward. It governs the heart and circulatory system. It also influences the functioning of the thymus gland and the immune system.

◆ **Energy of the heart chakra** – The one whose heart chakra has been opened radiates joy and friendliness. He will be considerate of others and have a highly developed sense of empathy.

◆ **Stones for the chakra** – Stones recommended for treating the heart chakra are green and pink. Green: aventurine, chrysocolla, chrysopras, jade, moss agate, olivine, emerald and tourmaline. Pink: coral, rhodonite, rhodochrosite and rose quartz.

◆ **Color for the chakra** – Green. The calming vibrations of the green spectrum are the best healing agents for the nervous system.

Fifth Chakra – Throat Chakra

This chakra lies at the base of the throat. It opens down and to the front. It provides energy to the thyroid gland. It also governs hunger and thirst, ear, eyes, nose and throat, the bronchial passages and the lungs, esophagus, vocal chords and speech.

◆ **Energy of the fifth chakra** – When energy flows freely through the throat chakra one will be open to new experiences. Such individuals will be able to express themselves and stand up for their beliefs.

◆ **Stones for the chakra** – Stones recommended for treating the throat chakra are aquamarine, chalcedony, celestine, chrysocolla, moonstone, opal, pearl, turquoise and blue topaz.

◆ **Color for the chakra** – Blue. The vibratory effect of the color blue is cooling, calming and healing. Blue is the color of innocence.

Symbol for the fifth chakra, the throat chakra

Sixth Chakra – Forehead Chakra, the Third Eye

The forehead chakra, or the third eye, lies above the top of the nose. It is linked to the eyes, nose, face and senses, as well as those more intangible avenues of perception, including insight and intuition.

◆ **Energy of the forehead chakra** – When energy flows through the forehead chakra one's understanding becomes broad and deep. Such an individual sees the world and himself clearly. He can rely upon his own intuitive sense.

◆ **Stones for the chakra** – Stones recommended for treating the third eye are sodalite, amethyst, sapphire, rock crystal and fluorite.

◆ **Color for the chakra** – Indigo. Indigo, the color of mysteries and mysticism, banishes sickness and evil from one's awareness and allows space for mental freedom.

Symbol for the sixth chakra, the third eye

The Seventh Chakra – Crown Chakra

Celestial energy enters the body through the crown chakra. It is the stepping off point for the infinite. It governs one's size and inner development.

◆ **Energy of the seventh chakra** – The opening of this chakra leads to enlightenment.

◆ **Stones for the chakra** – Stones recommended for treating the seventh chakra are amethyst, rock crystal, diamonds and violet fluorite.

◆ **Colors for the chakra.** Three colors are associated with the crown chakra. Violet, the color with the highest vibratory frequency; white, the color of pure intelligence; and gold, the light of the life force.

Symbol for the seventh chakra, the crown chakra

The Most Important Healing Stones

Learn about the most important, most popular and most beautiful healing stones. Discover their many different healing powers. Here more than 140 gemstones and minerals are described in detail.

The Variety of Stones

Since ancient times, natural medicine has made use of the healing powers of gemstones and crystals. Most of these stones exist in three different forms.

Rough stones: The most natural form is the unworked stone, broken from the rock and preserving its irregular, rough, untouched surface.

Tumbled stones: The rounded, tumbled stone without points or sharp edges feels smooth and pleasant to the touch and clearly reveals the mineral veins in the stone.

Jewelry: The third form is the cut gemstone. This is available cut in a rounded cabochon shape or faceted with many tiny little adjacent surfaces at an angle to each other, or with the flawless classical brilliant cut.

Different Healing Powers

Hundreds of gemstones and crystals are available in the market. Many of these stones exist in numerous sub-types or color variations. The deviations in crystal structure and in the colors or combinations of colors depend on where the piece was found. It is true that the crystal structure is always the same with a given type of stone, but the color may change depending on the metallic or mineral elements that a specimen may contain. An example is jasper, which is found in several colors including red, yellow, brown, and green.

All naturally created stones have healing powers, but not every stone works with the same intensity. Equally, not every stone is suitable for every kind of problem. Learn here about the most important healing stones in more detail. Find out where they are found, their appearance and their curative effects as well as their possible uses and applications. The following pages describe all the stones that play a particularly important role in healing with gemstones. These more important healing stones are treated in great detail. Some stones to which only moderate healing powers are attributed or that are not particularly interesting or popular are dealt with together in related groups.

Healing stones exist in various forms, including rough stones, tumbled stones and jewelry. They are also found in many color variations, depending on the traces of metals and minerals that they contain.

Actinolite

History and legend

The name actinolite is made up of the two Greek words *aktis* meaning "ray" and *lithos* meaning "stone." Literally translated it means "radiating stone." The name is inspired by the stone's radial structure. Actinolite is used mainly as a healing stone and is only rarely used as a gemstone in jewelry.

Healing properties

Actinolite is particularly effective in stimulating the inner organs such as the liver and the kidneys. In addition it also supports and promotes the general anabolic and growth processes in the body. If used in the form of quartz, actinolite will stimulate the body's metabolism and improve detoxification and elimination.

Actinolite is used to treat metabolic problems

Actinolite also affects the psyche: it promotes the sense of

self-esteem, improves inner harmony and encourages the purposefulness of the wearer.

Magical properties
No particular magical properties.

Chakra classification
Actinolite is particularly effective on the solar plexus.

Star sign
Not connected with any particular star sign.

Application and care
Because the stone works very slowly it should be worn directly on the skin over a long period.

Actinolite may be used as a rough stone, a touchstone or as a pendant.

Where found	Australia, China, Germany, Italy, Scotland, Norway, Uganda, Tanzania
Color(s)	green, white, gray; the stone varies from transparent to opaque; colorless
Chemical composition	$Ca_2(Mg,Fe^{2+})_5[(OH)|Si_4O_{11}]_2$
Hardness	5.5 to 6
Available forms	rough stone, touchstone, pendant
Crystallization	monoclinic crystal; flattened prismatic or oblong crystals

Actinolite can strengthen the liver and kidneys. Actinolite quartz helps the body to detoxify and stimulates the metabolism.

Agate

History and legend

The name is said to be derived from that of the river Achates in Sicily. The Greek philosopher Theophrastus (372–287 B.C.) described this gem as early as 300 B.C. and in Byzantium people already knew how to enhance the color of agate by burning.

Healing powers

Since time immemorial agate has been used during pregnancy for both mother and child, alleviating the discomfort experienced on certain days during pregnancy. It is used to treat headaches, dizziness, and impaired balance as well as skin problems. It is important that the stone should be in contact with the skin near the organ that needs healing. When placed on the heart and/or throat chakra, it combats feverish infections. Tired or inflamed eyes may also be alleviated by applying a disk of agate to them.

Agates are among the oldest good luck and healing stones.

Magical properties
Agate enables the wearer to choose between true friends and false ones. It is said to avert storms and lightning, protect children from danger, bring prosperity and prevent miscarriages.

Chakra classification
Red agates are related to the solar plexus chakra; blue agates are associated with the throat chakra.

Star signs
Recommended for Taurus and Capricorns to sensitize and strengthen willpower. Also appropriate for Scorpios.

Application and use
Agate should be worn directly on the skin. Once a month it should be cleansed under warm running water. The sun increases its energy.

Agate was the stone used to make the famous ancient Egyptian scarabs.

Because of its layered structure, agate was often used for the cameo engraving of heads and coats of arms against a deeper underlying color.

Where found	former volcanic regions; Black Forest, Saxony, Germany; in Brazil, Uruguay, Mexico, USA, Indian peninsula
Color(s)	from gray-blue to beige, reddish to brown, usually arranged in layers, in multiple stripes, patterns and decorative shapes
Chemical composition	SiO_2 + Al, Ca, Fe, Mn
Hardness	6.5 to 7
Available forms	pendant; polished stone for laying on the body or as a touchstone; as beads in necklaces; cut for display
Crystallization	formed in cavities made in lava by expanding gases; chalcedony quartz, crystallized out in small trigonal shapes; trigonal crystal

Alabaster

History and legend

An important healing stone, alabaster, a form of gypsum, has been used in naturopathy for hundreds of years. But it is also used in traditional medicine. The ancient Greeks and Romans had already recognized the special properties of gypsum or plaster to make impressions and casts: when mixed with water, plaster becomes as hard as stone. Alabaster and gypsum also have practical uses outside medicine, in particular playing an important part in building.

Alabaster crystals have a strongly purifying effect on the vegetative nervous system.

Healing properties

Alabaster crystals help tension, headache, lack of concentration and painful joints. They can also be used to alleviate hormonal imbalance. Psychologically alabaster can prevent outbursts of emotion and strengthen concentration.

Chakra classification

Alabaster crystals are particularly good for using on the root and sacral chakras. In order to stimulate and harmonize the root chakra, lie on your stomach and place the alabaster crystal on your lower back. To activate the sacral chakra, lie completely relaxed on your back and place the alabaster crystal directly on your skin about three inches below your navel.

Star sign

Alabaster crystals are not related to any particular star sign.

Application and care

Alabaster crystals should be discharged and cleansed once a month under warm running water.

Alabaster is named after the Egyptian town Alabastron.

Alabaster crystals in the form of selenite are special healing stones for the sexual organs and for use during pregnancy.

Where found	in all desert regions
Color(s)	white, gray to black (transparent); alabaster may also be yellowish, reddish or sand colored
Chemical composition	$CaSO_4 + 2H_2O$
Hardness	1.5 to 2
Available forms	another name for alabaster is gypsum, a hydrated calcium sulphate from which plaster is made; alabaster found in commerce consists mostly of single crystals and also of deformities
Crystallization	alabaster is hydrated calcium sulphate; monoclinic-prismatic crystallization

Alexandrite

History and legend
This small stone is rarely larger than the nail of the little finger. It was named after the Russian tsar, Alexander II (1818–81). It is one of the rarest gemstones, appearing on the precious stone market very infrequently.

Healing properties
This stone has a particularly positive effect on the nervous system. As a result it also has a beneficial effect on all the internal organs, ensuring their smooth, harmonious functioning. The organs that benefit most are the stomach, spleen, and pancreas. Alexandrite also has protective properties: it guards against hyperpepsia of the stomach and acidemia of the blood.

In addition, it has an extremely positive influence on the psyche.

Alexandrite is a member of the chrysoberyl group.

Alexandrite promotes inner harmony, joy and cheerfulness in the wearer. It also has a harmonizing effect on relationships.

Chakra classification
Alexandrite grounds the sacral chakra and promotes the flow of energy through it.

Star sign
Not associated with any particular star sign.

Application and care
Alexandrite should be cleansed under warm running water. After cleansing it should be re-energized by leaving it in the sun for a while.

Alexandrite helps the wearer find his inner center during meditation.

Where found	small areas of Brazil and Sri Lanka, former Soviet Unions
Color(s)	green/red, gray, greenish; the stone changes its color according to the light falling on it: it is green in daylight and red under artificial light
Chemical composition	$BeAl_2O_4$
Hardness	8.5
Available forms	rough crystal, pendant, cabochon, faceted gemstone
Crystallization	orthorhombic crystal

One the rarest gemstones in the world, alexandrite has the unique characteristic of appearing green in daylight and glowing red in artificial light.

Amazonite

History and legend
The naturalist Alexander von Humboldt (1769–1859) reported that people along the Rio Negro in Brazil wore amulets made of amazonite, which came from the land of the "women without men," the legendary country of the Indian amazons. In the 18th century amazonite was described as "green feldspar."

Healing properties
Amazonite is used to treat heart trouble and metabolic disorders. Placed on the third chakra it lifts depression and reduces anxiety; a necklace of amazonite worn directly on the skin will also alleviate headaches and migraines. Amazonite has a calming effect, corrects mood swings and helps the wearer come to terms with grief. It promotes confidence, vitality and joy of life. Placed under the pillow it promotes a restorative sleep.

Amazonite is a member of the family of rock-forming minerals.

Magical properties

Amazonite is often used in fortune-telling techniques such as the tarot and runes and stimulates powers of clairvoyance. Worn as an amulet it protects against snake bites and a wide range of diseases. In Egypt it was considered a holy stone.

Chakra classification

Placed on the heart and throat chakras, amazonite stimulates the artistic and creative side of its possessor. It also rids him of meanness, greed, and selfishness while making him tolerant and patient.

Star sign

Promotes vitality in Aquarians.

Application and care

Amazonite may be held or worn. It is also an excellent essence stone: place in a covered glass filled with water, leave overnight and drink in small amounts during the following day. Cleanse the stone once a week under warm running water, then leave in the sun for one hour.

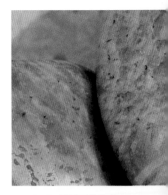

For the Indians of Brazil amazonite was a holy stone as well as a healing one.

Amazonite helps relieve all aches and pains, including neuralgia. It eases cramp and stress. Flat pieces of amazonite placed on the back and neck will relieve tension.

Where found	USA, Madagascar, former Soviet Union, South-West Africa, Brazil
Color(s)	green, blue-green as a result of traces of copper
Chemical composition	$K[AlSi_3O_8]$
Hardness	6 to 6.5
Available forms	for laying on the body, as a pendant, as a necklace
Crystallization	a potash mineral of the feldspar family and prismatically crystallized; trigonal crystal

Amber

History and legend

It was already known in antiquity that amber develops an attractive force on wooden shavings and straw when rubbed. The Persian name *kahrabâ*, "the attractor of straw," is inspired by this particular property. The Greeks called it *elektron*, meaning "sun-gold." The English name amber is derived from the Arab name for this stone "al-'anbar."

Healing properties

For 7,000 years amber has been used to stimulate the metabolism and treat skin ailments caused by a metabolic imbalance. Because of its warmth it is also used in the treatment of asthma. Allergic respiratory problems (such as allergy to cat fur) are greatly eased by wearing an amber necklace. Amber is also good for treating rheumatism and strengthening the heart muscles. It

Amber arouses joie de vivre *and a feeling of well-being in the wearer.*

even helps with epilepsy. Ground amber is used in the treatment of infections and boils. It enhances the powers of self-healing and promotes decisiveness.

Magical properties
Gold-colored amber symbolizes success.

Chakra classification
Amber is particularly effective on the navel chakra.

Star sign
It is the stone of Geminis, Leos and Virgos.

Application and care
Cleanse under lukewarm running water, when you notice that it only warms slowly when you wear it or hold it. Negative energy can make amber cloudy. Never leave amber in the sun because this may make it brittle.

If possible, amber should be worn directly on the skin.

Where found	Baltic coast, Lithuania, Poland, Germany, Dominican Republic (where the color range is slightly different)
Color(s)	light yellow to reddish-brown, also white, blue, greenish
Chemical composition	about 75 % C, 10 % H, 15 % O + S
Hardness	2 to 2.5
Available forms	rough stone, touchstone, bead necklace, fragment necklace, sphere, pendant; imitations are made from young resinous trees (copal)
Crystallization	fossil resin of the amber pine, petrified over a period of 50 million years; organic origin, not a mineral; amorphous form, usually bulbous; amorphous stone

Up to 3,000 different inclusions have been found in amber objects. These range from beetles and flies to spiders and water drops attached to the resin in primeval times and then petrified with it.

Amethyst

History and legend
The name is derived from the Greek word *amethyein*, meaning "not drunk." The Greeks wore an amethyst for protection against magic, homesickness, evil thoughts, and drunkenness. This is why wine was preferably served in amethyst beakers. Buddhist monks in India use amethyst to help them meditate. Hildegard von Bingen used amethysts with success to treat skin blemishes and tumors, and to ensure soft facial skin. Placed under one's pillow, it prevents nightmares.

Healing properties

Amethysts have a soothing, relaxing effect and promote healthy sleep.

When worn, the amethyst will alleviate migraines. Nervous headaches soon subside when a cross-section or geode of an amethyst is placed in the room. Amethyst also improves concentration.

Magical properties
Amethyst is said to attract justice and protect against burglars and thieves. It also wards off danger and violent death.

Chakra classification
Placed on the crown chakra or top of the head during meditation, amethyst increases concentration and confidence in life. People who regularly wear an amethyst necklace are said to fascinate others with their personality and charisma.

Star sign
Amethyst, the stone of Pisces, brings clarity to the conscious and unconscious mind.

Application and care
To cleanse it, wash it once a month under warm running water and leave overnight among dry hematite stones. Do not expose to the sun.

Amethysts are used to treat swellings, insect bites, and acne.

Where found	Brazil, Uruguay, Mexico, Western Australia, Morocco
Color(s)	violet, light to dark through iron inclusions
Chemical composition	SiO_2 + (Al, Ca, Fe, Li, Mg, Na)
Hardness	7
Available forms	touchstone, pendant, necklace, geode, cross-section, rough stone
Crystallization	formed from quartz crystal; appears as large crystals, usually in volcanic gas cavities; crystallized in hexagonal prisms; pointed on top: male crystal; flattened: female; trigonal crystal

In antiquity amethysts were also known as "stones of Bacchus," because out of jealousy the goddess Diana had changed a nymph with whom Bacchus had fallen in love into an amethyst.

Ametrine

History and legend
Ametrine used to be known only to the nomadic tribes of South America. Because it is not particularly beautiful, being contained within rather unattractive, brittle amethyst-quartz crystals, it was not considered very important. Through a freak of nature, it contains sectors of two gemstones, amethyst and citrine, in the same crystal.

Healing properties
Ametrine strengthens the nerves, promotes the supply of oxygen to the body and encourages the healing process after serious illnesses. The stone stimulates the activity of the brain and enhances the wearer's emotional life and creativity. It also combats hardening of the arteries and senile dementia, reduces deafness and helps cure eye complaints. Worn round the neck, near

Ametrine should be worn with gold or silver.

the thyroid gland, it reduces trembling, sweating and blushing. Ametrine symbolizes growth; it promotes maturity and encourages a more confident attitude towards life. The stone is also said to have a soothing effect on the soul and create inner harmony in the wearer. It influences the needs and wishes of the individual and helps resolve inner contradictions.

Ametrine is one of the rarest and most valuable gemstones.

Chakra classification
Ametrine is related to the crown chakra or top of the head and the root chakra. It should be used with caution during meditation; it greatly enhances concentration as well as intuition, but if used for too long a period, can lead to inner imbalances.

Star sign
Particularly suited to Virgos and Libras.

Application and care
The stone should be cleansed every week under warm running water. It is then charged among a mass of amethyst crystals or geodes. Ametrine is best able to manifest its powers when worn with gold or silver.

Ametrine is made up of two powerful gemstones: amethyst and citrine. It has a very soothing effect on the soul and brings inner harmony and equilibrium to the wearer.

Where found	Brazil and Bolivia (very rare)
Color(s)	violet, golden, translucent
Chemical composition	SiO_2 + (Al, Ca, Fe, Li, Mg, Na)
Hardness	7
Available forms	rough or tumbled stone, pendant and necklace as well as faceted stones, touchstone, sphere
Crystallization	it is a silica quartz with traces of aluminum and iron; the stone is a combination of citrine and amethyst — hence the name; trigonal crystal

Andalusite

History and legend
The name of this stone is derived from the place where it is found. It was discovered in Spain in Andalusia before the birth of Christ. Since time immemorial the yellowish andalusite has been recognized as one of the most important and effective healing stones. According to Greek tradition it was renamed chiastolite or "cross stone" because when polished it displays the shape of the Greek letter Chi and the Latin letter X in its cross-section.

Healing properties
The ancient Greeks used Andalusite for healing and decorative purposes.

Andalusite is ideal for the treatment of uncontrollable movements because it influences the muscles and nerves through its effect on the brain. It regulates sleep and can alleviate the paralysis of nerves, muscles, and joints. It also affects the psyche, encouraging the process of psychological maturation and independence.

Magical Properties

Andalusite symbolizes independence and was already considered a powerful healing stone in antiquity.

Chakra classification

When placed on the solar plexus chakra, it promotes a desire for self-realization. It helps the wearer identify problems and energy blockages while at the same time pointing to their resolution. It is particularly powerful when used in conjunction with natural citrine or diamond.

Star sign

Not associated with any particular star sign.

Application and care

Andalusite should be cleansed twice a month under warm running water and charged by being placed for two hours in the sun among rock crystals. If it turns cloudy, it should be placed overnight in a glass of water together with a few hematite stones.

Andalusite should be worn directly on the skin and held in the hand.

Where found	USA (California), Brazil, France, Sweden, Spain, Sri Lanka
Color(s)	brown-yellowish crystal, cruciform cross-section
Chemical composition	$Al_2[O/SiO_4]$ + C, Ca, Cr, Fe, K Mg, Mn, Ti
Hardness	6 to 7.5
Available forms	as a jewel, or for use as a rough or tumbled stone
Crystallization	cruciform cross-section; it has sparkling inclusions formed from carboniferous substances; orthorhombic crystal

Andalusite protects against arthritis, rheumatism and inflammation of the joints. It alleviates painful diseases of the tissues while also healing the skin and connective tissues.

Andes opal

History and legend

This "stone of hope" was discovered in the Andes during the wars between the Indian peoples of Central and South America. The Incas and Aztecs believed this stone to be the eyes of their gods, abandoned by them when they were forced to leave the earth. The stone is a reminder that in nature people and animals should live together in harmony.

Healing properties

In Peru the Andes opal is worshipped as a protective and healing stone.

The pink Andes opal affects the enzymes in the body which regulate its metabolic processes and vegetative functions. Diseases, psychological problems and strong allergic reactions usually appear when the enzymes in the body have become unbalanced. The green-blue Andes opal reduces the allergic reactions of the tissues. It also has a powerful effect on the respiratory organs and is

therefore ideally suited for the treatment of respiratory problems, caused by allergic reactions to environmental pollution, dust, animal hair or ozone. Worn round the neck it can alleviate hay fever. If patted on the skin like water, it soothes skin rashes and skin irritations. It is also used in the treatment of laryngitis, serious hoarseness and loss of voice. It is known to reduce stress-related anxieties. The brown and white varieties of Andes opal have little effect on the body. All Andes opals are, however, very helpful for calming nerves during examinations, removing mental blocks and strengthening the memory.

Chakra classification

The pink Andes opal increases sexual potency when placed on the root chakra. The blue-green Andes opal is most effective when placed on the heart chakra and throat chakra.

Star sign

Not associated with any particular star sign.

Application and care

The Andes opal should be cleansed once a month under warm running water, then charged for several hours during the night among rock crystals. The white Andes opal removes the damaging rays from the colored opals. That is why this opal should not be cleansed. It should, however, be charged overnight among rock crystals twice a month if possible.

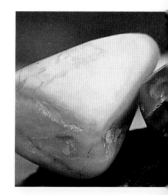

The pink Andes opal is said to be very helpful in the treatment of depression.

The Andes opal can be worn round the neck as a necklace or pendant. It can also be drunk as a tea. In that form, it will help prevent viral infections, ticks and worms.

Where found	only in the Peruvian Andes
Color(s)	pink, blue, green, brown, white
Chemical composition	$SiO_2 + H_2O$
Hardness	6 to 7
Available forms	rough stone, touchstone, sphere, pyramid, necklace, pendant
Crystallization	amorphous stone

Antimony

History and legend

According to tradition antimony was much appreciated in antiquity where it was applied on the neck or the eyes for healing purposes. It was already known then to have a healing effect on the sexual organs. Antimony was also used for cosmetic purposes: it was used in powder form as eye shadow on the eyelids.

Healing properties

Antimony helps in alleviating skin ailments including neurodermatitis, psoriasis, skin rashes, and eczema. It also regulates the digestion and alleviates digestive problems such as heartburn and nausea.

The stone also has a beneficial effect on the psyche. It makes it easier for the wearer to establish boundaries, to concentrate on and take care of himself. In addition, it has a cheering and

Antimony is found in a variety of shades of gray through to black.

revitalizing effect: it drives away bad moods, increases creativity, and it helps a person to handle his own feelings better.

Chakra classification
Antimony works best on the solar plexus chakra.

Star sign
Not associated with any particular star sign.

Application and care
This stone should never be cleansed with water. Instead, place it overnight in a bowl filled with hematite stones and then charge it again by placing it in the sun.

In antiquity antimony was used on the eyelids as eye shadow.

Where found	Japan, as well as in Romania, USA, Borneo
Color(s)	gray; also in various shades of gray ranging from blue-gray, bluish steel gray or black
Chemical composition	Sb_2S_3 + Fe, Cu, Pb, Zn + (Ag, Au, Co)
Hardness	2
Available forms	rough stone
Crystallization	prismatic orthorhombic, spearlike, radial, undulating twinned crystal

Antimony's medical virtues were known in antiquity. It was applied on the neck, eyes, and sexual organs for healing purposes.

Apache's tears

History and legend

According to the Indian legend that tells the story of the origin of this stone's name, the white men who arrived in the New World wanted more and more land and "bought" off the native inhabitants with weapons and alcohol to get it. The Apaches, seduced by these new temptations, were soon driven further out of their land by the new "inhabitants." Finally,robbed of their entire birthright and grief-stricken, they began to cry. Their tears fell to the ground where they solidified, signs of their enduring sorrow. These transparent Apache's tears belong to the obsidian family. Today these stones are still considered a symbol of freedom, power, and health by all Native American tribes.

Healing properties

Apache's tears are used to alleviate poor digestion, gastric

Apache's tears reduce and cure apathy and psychological disorders.

problems and intestinal disorders, especially when these are stress related. They soothe stomach upset. Apache's tears stimulate the body's own production of vitamins B and E. This contributes to healthy consistency of the blood and improves the function of the skin.

The psyche is also influenced by Apache's tears: they relieve depression and anxiety about the future. In addition, the wearer will experience a greater joy in life and a more harmonious emotional state.

Chakra classification
Apache's tears can be used on all chakras.

Star sign
Not associated with any particular star sign.

Application and care
Apache's tears should be washed in a bowl of warm water once a month. Their power is even greater when the stones are recharged among rock crystals.

Today Apache's tears are only found on a few Indian reservations in the Western United States, in the states of Arizona and Utah.

These mostly round or oval obsidians are actually volcanic rock glass, created by the sudden cooling of drops of lava coming into contact with water or ice.

Where found	Arizona and Utah
Color(s)	black, translucent; different color effects from traces of different metals such as iron, titanium, manganese
Chemical composition	Effusive rock
Hardness	7
Available forms	touchstone, pendant
Crystallization	amorphous

Apatite

History and legend
The name is derived from the Greek *apatáo*, meaning "I am mistaken," because for a long time it was confused with other stones. The stone has a hardness factor of 5 so it can easily be identified by a "scratch test." Stones that might be confused with it such as aquamarine and beryl are harder. Apatite was not yet known in ancient mythology, its often fascinating strong blue color only became famous in modern times (it also exists in white, yellow, green and orange). Consequently nothing is known of earlier applications for healing purposes.

Apatite has a high concentration of minerals and trace elements.

Healing properties
Apatite is said to mobilize energy reserves for the healthy formation of bones, cells, and teeth. It is therefore used to treat arthrosis, painful joints and bone fractures, and for children during their

growing years. Eye trouble can also be relieved by the application of apatite.

Magical properties
Apatite encourages intuition during meditation and can stimulate "memories of past lives."

Chakra classification
When placed on the throat chakra, apatite produces a feeling of warmth and harmony and helps in overcoming problems.

Star sign
Apatite is assigned to Aquarius.

Application and care
In order to make apatite water, the stone should be placed in still mineral water for twelve hours, covered with a lid. It should be cleansed once a week in warm running water. It should be placed in the sun to be recharged. It is an easy stone to look after.

As well as gray-blue, apatite is also found in blue-violet, white, yellow, green, and orange colors.

Apatite has a particularly beneficial effect on the functions of the small intestine because of its high mineral content.

Where found	Sri Lanka, Burma, India, Canada, Mexico, Brazil
Color(s)	blue-violet, white, yellow, orange and green
Chemical composition	$Ca_5[(F,OH,Cl)|(PO_4)_3]$
Hardness	5
Available forms	rough stone, tumbled stone, touchstone, pendant, crystal, sphere
Crystallization	belongs to the family of phosphate minerals and usually crystallizes opaque (dull) or occasionally clear; hexagonal crystal structure, thick layered with a rich surface; hexagonal-bipyramidal crystal

Apophyllite

History and legend
This stone has not been known for a long time. Its cleavage points have a mother-of-pearl luster.

Healing properties
This stone is used to treat asthma and cure diseases of the respiratory tract. It is also beneficial in the treatment of skin disorders and allergies. Apophyllite is said to stimulate the heart by increasing the supply of oxygen, while at the same time eliminating deposits and waste and correcting deficiencies in tissues and blood vessels.

Apophyllite also has a beneficial effect on the psyche: it is said to help with depression and psychological blocks, giving confidence and courage to its possessor while making him more sociable and cheerful.

Apophyllite is one of the most powerful protective and healing stones.

Magical properties

The stone is said to have saving properties. The light-colored apophyllite symbolizes the light at the end of a dark tunnel full of dangers and worries.

Chakra classification

Placed on the heart chakra, apophyllite relieves tension in the nervous system and promotes relaxation.

Star sign

This stone is particularly suitable for Geminis.

Application and care

This stone is cleansed under warm running water. After cleansing it is charged again in a glass of water together with green tourmaline or aventurine or among rock crystals.

Apophyllite from India is especially beautiful.

Where found	Iceland, Norway, also India and Brazil
Color(s)	various shades of green ranging from light green to emerald green, white and pink, translucent
Chemical composition	$KCa_4[F|(Si_4O_{10})_2]\cdot8H_2O$
Hardness	4.5 to 5
Available forms	crystal, aggregate crystals
Crystallization	hydrated layered silicate, very good energy conductor; tetragonal crystal

The name apophyllite is derived from the Greek apophyllein which means "flaking off." Under intensive heat it breaks entirely into flakes.

Aquamarine

History and legend
Legend has it that aquamarine originally came from a mermaid's jewelry box (Latin *aqua maris* means "sea water"). It is said to bring pure love. By turning darker or lighter, the stone indicates what is true and false. When it becomes almost white, it is said to warn against false friends.

Healing properties
This stone is placed on the neck or worn as a short necklace to treat neck and throat problems. When placed on the third chakra it relaxes the solar plexus and digestive organs. It also protects against seasickness. A large aquamarine placed in water overnight and used the following morning to wash the skin without rubbing too vigorously will alleviate allergies. Placed on swollen glands or worn round the neck, it will reduce the swelling. Chronic tonsillitis

In the Middle Ages aquamarine was a symbol of chastity.

can be relieved by wearing a necklace of aquamarine together with turquoise, sodalite, chalcedony, and blue topaz. Aquamarine has a beneficial effect on the thyroid gland and is helpful in the treatment of problems with the vocal cords and speech.

Magical properties
Aquamarine symbolizes peace. It encourages a gentle nature and personality in the wearer.

Chakra classification
Depending on the color, aquamarine is related to the throat chakra.

Star sign
For Aquarius it promotes friendship and love, while for Pisces it encourages awareness. Libras are warned against danger.

Application and care
The stone must be worn directly on the skin if possible. It should be cleansed every day by holding briefly under running water. Place in the sun to charge after frequent use. A necklace can be cleansed by placing in a dry bowl overnight with hematite and aquamarine tumbled stones.

Hildegard von Bingen included aquamarine among her twelve healing stones.

Where found	Brazil, Madagascar, Ural, USA, Nigeria, Pakistan, Afghanistan
Color(s)	translucent light blue to sea green
Chemical composition	$Al_2Be_3[Si_6O_{18}]$
Hardness	7.5 to 8
Available forms	rough stone, crystal, touchstone, pendant, necklace, sphere, calming stone
Crystallization	crystallized in hexagonal prisms, it belongs to the beryl family and owes its color to inclusions of iron; hexagonal crystal

Aquamarine regulates the lymph system and blood circulation. It can also strengthen the immune system and thus protect against all types of colds and allergies.

Aragonite

History and legend

Aragonite was already known as a healing and decorative stone in Roman and Greek antiquity. It was named after the Spanish river Aragón. It is found near many thermal springs in the form of a marble-like stone. The Indians, Romans and Greeks loved this stone because it was easy to work with and polish and was therefore ideal for works of art and carvings.

Healing properties

Aragonite promotes the formation of healthy skin, bones, and tissue.

Aragonite promotes good bone formation and healthy joints because of its high calcium content. It should be carried on one's person as a touchstone. It is also said to strengthen the immune system, reduce hypersensitivity and prevent calcium deficiencies. It also has beneficial effects on the psyche: it has a soothing effect on the wearer's mood and promotes a peaceful way of life.

When placed under the pillow it protects against nightmares and sleepwalking. It removes nervousness in the wearer when dealing with other people.

Magical properties
As a marble stone, aragonite symbolizes power and strength.

Chakra classification
Aragonite works well on sacral chakra.

Star sign
Aragonite is not associated with any particular star sign.

Application and care
Rough and decorative stones are cleansed twice a month in warm water and charged overnight among rock crystals. Large uncut stones and spheres, placed in one's room, are particularly effective.

The healing power of aragonite was already known in ancient Greece.

Where found	Morocco, Italy, Germany
Color(s)	white, yellowish, red-brown, brown
Chemical composition	SiO_2 + Al, Ca, Fe, Mn
Hardness	3.5 to 4
Available forms	rough stone, touchstone, jewelry, doughnut, necklace, obelisk, pyramid, sphere, tumbled stone, table tops
Crystallization	it is a calcium carbonate and occurs in calciferous rocks; is often converted into calcite; orthorhombic-bipyramidal crystal

The yellow, green, pink and brown aragonite, also known as onyx, is used to make a wide range of items of practical use, works of art, and decorative objects.

Australian amulet stone

History and legend

Australia's native inhabitants, the Aborigines, worshipped Ayers Rock as the "Holy stone of Mother Earth," which they called Uluru in their own language. Carrying a piece of it on one's person was believed to protect the wearer and ward off all danger. The Aborigines called these amulet stones "Uluru's children." They were believed to ensure a harmonious relationship between all creatures, nature, and the earth. This "Trinity" is also reflected in the magical lines that mark the surface of the stone. This stone is extremely hard to find because it is extraordinarily rare and highly sought after.

"Uluru's children" are found near Ayers Rock.

Healing properties

Australian amulet stones cleanse the blood and give the wearer resistance and vitality. They also protect the connective tissue

and skin from disease, rashes, and eczema. They are said to alleviate migraine, painful joints caused by weather conditions, and cure diseases of the lining of the stomach. They have a beneficial effect on the metabolism and circulation by working on the vegetative nervous system.

Amulet stones also protect against depression and prevent anger and outbreaks of rage. They increase the wearer's sense of equilibrium, harmony, and joy. Negative energy is converted into positive vibrations.

Chakra classification
The amulet stone works well on all chakras.

Star sign
Not associated with any particular star sign.

Application and care
The stone should be discharged and cleansed once a month under warm running water. Exposure to the sun is also very effective.

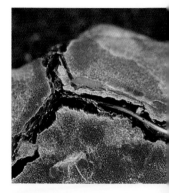

Amulet stones are passed down in one's family and "stroked" in case of need.

Up to this day scientists cannot explain the origin of amulet stones because they are a completely different stone from those of the site where they are found.

Where found	only in Australia, at Ayers Rock (the oldest rock in the world)
Color(s)	agate-colored, with some lines running round the stone
Chemical composition	SiO_2
Hardness	7
Available forms	rough stone
Crystallization	trigonal crystal

Aventurine

History and legend

In ancient Greece aventurine was sewn into the clothes of men going to war to preserve their courage and optimism. It is said to enhance the sense of humor and cheerfulness of its possessor.

Healing properties

Aventurine has a beneficial effect on many skin irritations, acne, allergies, suppurating wounds but also flaking skin, dandruff and hair loss. Cover the stone with water, leave overnight, and then wash the skin and hair with it. This water can also be used to bathe strained eyes that will greatly benefit from it. Worn as an amulet, it can be used to relieve pain.

Aventurine relieves deep-seated anxieties and promotes relaxation and recuperation.

Aventurine also has an effect on the psyche: it strengthens an individual sense of self. It is the ideal stone for those who are looking for a positive view of life.

Magical properties
Aventurine symbolizes tranquillity and patience. It gives the wearer inner equilibrium and stimulates dreaming.

Chakra classification
Placed on the heart chakra it removes anxiety and helps in the treatment of psychosomatic disorders, even those that have plagued the wearer since childhood.

Star sign
Particularly suitable for Cancer but also Taurus and Sagittarius.

Application and care
The stone should be worn either for a long time or, in the case of acute illnesses, taped onto the affected part of the body. Cleanse once a month under running water and recharge in the sun.

Blue quartz is also known as blue aventurine.

Where found	Brazil, South Africa, Urals, Siberia and India
Color(s)	shimmering light green, sometimes with glittering inclusions of chrome mica, from which its color comes; the more light the stone receives, the more beautiful its colors are
Chemical composition	$SiO_2 + KAl_2 [(OH, F)_2/Al\ Si_3O_{10}] + (Cr)$
Hardness	7
Available forms	rough stone for placing on the body; polished for laying on the body or as a touchstone, cut for jewelry
Crystalli- zation	Aventurine is a solid quartz with a trigonal crystal structure

Blue quartz or blue aventurine alleviates headaches and migraines as well as helping in the treatment of influenza and colds. Blue quartz spheres protect against radiation.

Azurite

History and legend

The name is derived from the Persian word *lazhward*, which means the color blue. The ancient Greeks and Romans used ground azurite for medicinal purposes and as a dye. Solomon's books mention a stone that contained copper and it is thought, although not with absolute certainty, that this stone might be azurite. The proverbial justice of this biblical king is said to have been strengthened during meditation with this stone.

Healing properties

Azurite stimulates the thyroid gland and promotes growth in children.

Azurite is said to promote and speed up the healing of general wounds and post-operative wounds. It soothes the nerves and prevents internal blockages and congestion. The stone stimulates the activity of the liver and, as a result, detoxifies the body.

On a psychological level, it is said to increase concentration and sharpen the wearer's sense of justice. It eases the process of decision making and promotes critical thinking.

Magical properties
Azurite symbolizes insight and discovery and promotes a sense of justice.

Chakra classification
It works particularly well on the forehead and crown chakras.

Star sign
Especially good for Capricorns.

Application and care
The stone should be cleansed once month by placing overnight among tumbled hematite stones. This energy-rich stone does not need charging.

Azurite is the stone of knowledge and discovery

Dark blue azurite with its striking color has been known since the very early days of mining. Ground azurite was not only used for medicinal purposes but also as a pigment: azure blue.

Where found	Morocco, Arizona, Black Forest (Germany)
Color(s)	dark blue
Chemical composition	$Cu_3 [(OH)_2/(CO_3)_2]$
Hardness	3.5 to 4
Available forms	rough stone, touchstone, spheres, crystal, cabochon, pendant (rarely)
Crystalli-zation	it is a basic copper carbonate that is found in beds of copper ore; monoclinic crystal

Azurite-malachite

History and legend

The Indians believe that azurite-malachite is the stone that protects the earth: it protects nature, animals, and people, and it is the divine link between heaven and earth. Because of its strong magical link with heaven, the water rains back down on earth. The green coloring in the stone represents life on earth, while the blue symbolizes life in the water.

Healing properties

Azurite-malachite protects and supports the detoxifying organs in the body. It has a beneficial effect in the fight against kidney stones, gallstones, and liver disease. It has a positive effect on the nervous system and muscles. Azurite-malachite is also believed to protect against radiation damage.

The stone is known to have a positive influence on the psyche:

Azurite-malachite combines the blue of azurite and the green of malachite.

those who have a weak character or suffer from mood swings will benefit greatly from this stone. Azurite-malachite creates a sense of well-being that is also felt by those around one. In addition, the stone is known to protect the general health of the wearer.

Chakra classification

Azurite-malachite should be placed on the forehead or heart chakra during meditation.

Star sign

Particularly good for Capricorns.

Application and care

Cleanse the stone only during the night in a bowl of tumbled hematite stones. The stone should only be cleansed when you notice that it only warms up slightly when worn on the body, or when it becomes discolored. It should be charged once a month by placing it overnight among rock crystals.

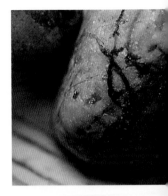

Azurite-malachite is a particularly gentle meditation and chakra stone.

Azurite-malachite is a copper mineral combining blue azurite and green malachite. These two precious stones, which are usually found close together in the same places, have grown into this beautiful stone as a result of extreme heat and very high pressure.

Where found	a small area in Arizona
Color(s)	dark blue with green inclusions
Chemical composition	$Cu_3[OH/CO_3]_2 + Cu_2[(OH)_2/CO_3]$
Hardness	3.5 to 4
Available forms	rough stone, touchstone, cabochon, sphere, pendant, necklace
Crystallization	monoclinic crystal

Barite

History and legend
Barite is a comparatively heavy stone. This is also reflected in its name, which is derived from the Greek word *barys*, meaning something like "very heavy." It was only discovered about two hundred years ago, in the early nineteenth century, when it was used as a healing and protective stone. In the twentieth century scientists discovered it had other properties. They found that the stone could protect against dangerous X-rays, ultra-violet radiation and radioactivity.

Barite is particularly useful for protecting children against the damage caused by the harmful rays of the sun.

Healing properties
Barite offers protection for those working with computers. As well as screening radiation, it also reduces the level of skin damage. It is therefore very helpful in cases of sunburn. Barite water is used to treat scaly, inflamed and irritated skin. It is also helpful in the

treatment of acne and spots or pimples on the face. Fungal infections of the nails and teeth can also benefit from being treated with barite. In addition, it has a beneficial effect on the psyche; it is therefore used to cure psychological problems such as obsessive-compulsive neurosis or compulsive behavior, such as agoraphobia or compulsive cleaning.

Chakra classification
Barite can be used on all chakras at the same time.

Application and care
Cleanse barite once a week under running warm water. It regenerates itself and therefore does not need to be recharged.

Long prism-shaped barite crystals are especially good at absorbing radiation.

Where found	Germany, Sweden, Italy, Mexico, Australia, USA, Brazil
Color(s)	white, gray, yellow, blue, pink, greenish; a translucent form is also sometimes found
Chemical composition	$BaSO_4$
Hardness	3 to 3.5
Available forms	rough stone, crystal; it is only rarely worked
Crystallization	orthorhombic crystal shape

Today barite is often used in industry to protect against all kinds of radiation, in the form of protective screens and protective clothing for instance.

Beryl

History and legend

Beryl originates from Mesopotamia and was worshipped as a magic stone by the ancient Hebrews. It was believed to strengthen the belief in God. The Bible says it will one day take its place in the walls of the New Jerusalem. But beryl also has other virtues: it is said to protect marital feelings and love. And it will help its possessors reach high positions.

Healing properties

To treat eye problems beryl should be placed on the closed eyelids in the evening. It is also used to alleviate less serious stomach and bowel disorders and to detoxify the body. It is helpful in the treatment of angina and when placed on the neck it can relieve the symptoms caused by long-term stress or traveling. It calms nervous excitement caused by traveling and homesickness. It

Beryl is a very gentle healer.

also enhances the appeal and erotic feelings of its possessor, especially if it is worn with morganite.

Magical properties

Beryl symbolizes protection; white beryl in particular should be worn as a protective stone whenever traveling.

Chakra classification

Beryl is ideal to open all chakras. It strengthens the magnetism of the wearer and gives him sex appeal and charm. When combined with morganite it acts as an aphrodisiac.

Star sign

Beryl is the stone of Gemini.

Application and care

It should always be placed overnight in a bowl with hematite tumbled stones and cleansed under warm running water while rubbing lightly.

The pink variant of beryl is called morganite.

Where found	Brazil, Madagascar, Pakistan, Afghanistan
Color(s)	colorless, golden yellow, yellow-green, white
Chemical composition	$Be_3Al_2 (Si_6O_{18})$ + Fe, K, Li, Mn, Na
Hardness	7.5 to 8
Available forms	commercially fairly rare; rough stone, tumbled stone, crystal, necklace, sphere
Crystallization	six-sided columnar prism, its color is caused by traces of foreign substances: yellow and gold by iron; when yellowish in color, it is often known as heliodor; hexagonal stone

The Greeks used the refracting property of beryl to make the first spectacles. At the time of Nero white beryl was found on the Island of Elba and it was then cut to make eyeglasses.

Biotite

History and legend

Biotite swells in the heat of summer and small lens-like pieces are produced from the inside of the stone. This explains why biotite is considered a powerful birthing stone. A smooth, round stone is pressed firmly in the fist of the woman giving birth to ease the process of labor. Biotite is a member of the mica family. Biotite disks are more effective medicinally than biotite lenses because their chemical composition is purer.

Healing properties

Biotite encourages the detoxification of the body. Applied on the body it is used to ease the pain caused by problems such as sciatica, rheumatism and gout. It is particularly popular as a protective and energizing stone during childbirth. It can either be placed on the pubic bone or held in the hand of the woman giving birth.

Biotite can be used to open up all the chakras.

Biotite reduces tension, stimulates the metabolism and promotes the purification of the body. It also encourages intuition and creativity. It is helpful in the treatment of stress-related disorders such as insomnia, depression and melancholy.

Magical properties
Biotite is considered the perfect stone for women: it eases childbirth and the pain associated with it.

Chakra classification
Biotite disks open up all chakras. They are particularly relaxing when placed on the navel chakra and the third eye.

Star sign
Not associated with any particular star sign.

Application and care
Biotite should be cleansed at regular intervals under warm running water. It must be left for several hours in direct sun to restore its former energy.

When used for healing purposes, pure biotite is required rather than biotite lenses.

Where found	Brazil, USA, Australia, South Africa, Russia, Norway
Color(s)	black with silver-gray mica
Chemical composition	$K (Fe, Mg, Mn)_3 [(OH, F)_2 AlSi_3O_{10}]$
Hardness	2 to 2.5
Available forms	Disks, lenses; accumulations of biotite around quartz feldspar
Crystallization	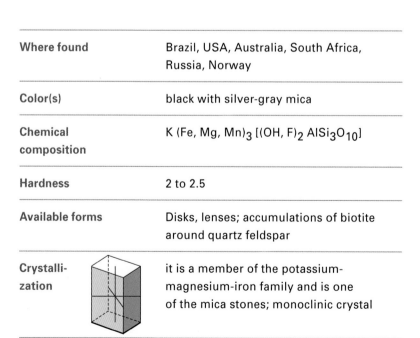 it is a member of the potassium-magnesium-iron family and is one of the mica stones; monoclinic crystal

Beware of false healing stones! They imitate the appearance of real biotite but inside they contain an impure crystal, feldspar quartz, that has unpredictable powers.

Brazilianite

History and legend

The primitive people of South America consider brazilianite a healing stone; they also used it as an amulet. This yellowish-green to light-green precious stone was only recognized as such in 1945. It takes its name from the place where it was found.

Healing properties

Brazilianite is a very rare healing stone. It is used in the treatment of disorders of the nervous system, brain, and spinal cord. It is therefore also an effective treatment for multiple sclerosis. The stone is said to cure the center of inflammation and protect the patient from further attacks of the disease. Brazilianite is also used to treat damage to nerve tissue, in particular when caused by pollution, pesticides, paint, or varnish.

Brazilianite also helps solve psychological problems by giving

In the past brazilianite was thought to be either green quartz or pale chrysoprase.

the wearer positive energy. The stone gives him *joie de vivre* and encourages self-expression. It strengthen the nerves and ensures that the organs work together harmoniously.

Chakra classification
The stone is most effective on the heart chakra and strengthens the spirit and soul.

Star sign
Not associated with any particular star sign.

Application and care
Only warm water, soap and ammonium chloride should be used to clean brazilianite jewelry. Brazilianite must be recharged in the sun or among rock crystals.

In Brazil, its country of origin, it has a long tradition of being worn as an amulet stone.

Where found	Minas Gerais (Brazil)
Color(s)	yellowish to light green
Chemical composition	$NaAl_3 [(OH)_2 / PO_4]_2$
Hardness	5.5 to 6
Available forms	brazilianite is available in various commercial forms, as a rough stone, a touchstone and as a jewel, especially in the form of a pendant; only rarely is the stone worked into jewelry
Crystallization	monoclinic crystal

This precious stone is only found in a very small part of central Brazil. As late as 1945 it was still thought to be green quartz or pale chrysoprase.

Breckzien jasper

History and legend

This stone is known as "variegated stone" in South Africa; its striking markings can be interpreted as fanciful landscapes, figures and extraordinary shapes. The imagination knows no bounds. Because of the stone's figurative motifs the Indians in Venezuela used it to find out about the past and see into the future. The Indians also believed that the stone ensured a happy marriage because it encouraged eternal love and fidelity.

Healing properties

The beautiful breckzien jasper is often used in jewelry.

Its healing powers are not so pronounced as those of the red jasper. It has blood-staunching properties and is also recommended in the treatment of sleep disorders, caused by earth radiation and water radiation. In this case a disk of breckzien jasper should be placed under the pillow. If the stone turns dark-

er, it confirms that there is radiation. You must then remove this radiation from the stone with a hematite sphere and move your bed. The stone can be worn as a necklace to prevent thyroid deficiencies. It also has beneficial effects on a psychological level: this stone helps the wearer to keep calm and not be irritated by his surroundings. It strengthens the body by reducing negative energies and stimulating positive energy, building up drive, courage, and the will to live.

Chakra classification
Penetrates best when placed on the solar plexus chakra.

Like red jasper, this jasper also has blood-staunching properties.

Star sign
The stone is most beneficial for Capricorns.

Application and care
Cleanse the stone once a month under warm running water. Charge the stone in the sun or among rock crystals.

Where found	all parts of the world; it is found in large quantities in Mexico, China, South Africa
Color(s)	red with black inclusions, opaque
Chemical composition	SiO_2
Hardness	7
Available forms	tumbled stone, touchstone, pendant, sphere
Crystallization	trigonal crystal

The stone consists mainly of red jasper with black inclusions, caused by the presence of manganese, iron, and hematite.

Bronzite

History and legend
The ancient Romans used to grind bronzite into powder form to protect against mental illness and mental confusion and as an effective treatment to strengthen the nerves. They also wore the stone as a protective amulet. Bronzite was highly valued by the Greeks and Romans as a decorative stone because of its particular brilliance. It was named bronzite because of its bronze-like appearance.

Healing properties
Bronzite helps in the treatment of cysts and is also used to treat skin disorders such as rashes, pimples, and eczema. It also relaxes tense muscles and muscular cramp. In addition, it combats premature aging and prevents the skin from dehydrating. The stone brings the wearer inner peace, removes stress, protects

The purest bronzite comes from Brazil.

against depressive moods and works favorably on the psyche. If the wearer suffers from psychological stress of a traumatic character, bronzite helps him to overcome the effects of agonizing memories.

Chakra classification
Bronzite is most effective when used on the forehead, but it can also be used on the solar plexus chakra.

Star sign
Not associated with any particular star sign.

Application and care
Bronzite should be cleansed once a month under warm running water. It should be recharged overnight among rock crystals.

Bronzite is an excellent stone for healing psychological trauma.

Where found	India, Western Australia, China, South Africa, Brazil
Color(s)	bronze colors with silvery traces
Chemical composition	$(Mg, Fe)_2 [Si_2O_6]$
Hardness	5 to 6
Available forms	this stone is widely available as a rough stone, also as a tumbled stone and as a touchstone in specialty shops
Crystallization	orthorhombic crystal system

Bronzite is also found in meteorites. This means that other worlds in our solar system must have a similar composition to that of the earth.

Calcite

History and legend
Native Americans consider calcite a holy stone of the land of their fathers that was given to them by the gods.

Healing properties
Itching, inflamed or suppurating skin can be treated and cured by applying an ointment consisting of fat (for instance petroleum jelly) and ground calcite. This stone symbolizes clarification and mental growth. Because of its high calcium content it is an excellent stone for treating bone disorders and has a very beneficial effect on the formation of bone. The stone is found in various colors including orange calcite, blue and green calcite, citrine calcite, and manganese calcite. It has different healing properties depending on the color of the stone. The white, salmon or pink-colored manganese calcite has a beneficial effect on the body fluids. Green

Calcite is found in several very different colors.

calcite is very good for the heart while the reddish-brown citrine calcite is excellent for the metabolism.

Magical properties
Calcite symbolizes inner enlightenment and mental growth. It promotes development, especially in children.

Chakra classification
Calcite works in different ways on the chakras, depending on its color. Blue calcite works particularly well on the throat chakra; green and pink calcites are highly effective on the heart chakra. The reddish-brown calcite should be used on the solar plexus.

Star sign
Green calcite is linked to Capricorns.

Application and care
The stone should be cleansed once a month under warm running water and charged overnight among rock crystals.

Calcite is one of the commonest minerals.

All calcites consist of almost pure calcium. Because of their high calcium content they are used mainly for the bones.

Where found	all over the world; certain color varieties are found in particular countries
Color(s)	yellow, orange, pink, brown, green and blue, frequently translucent
Chemical composition	$CaCO_3$ + Fe, Mn + (Co, Pb)
Hardness	3
Available forms	tumbled stone, pendant, powder
Crystallization	hydrated calcium carbonate; very soft; the color comes from mineral additions; more than 1,000 surface combinations

Carnelian

History and legend

Carnelian is one of the oldest gemstones and protective stones in history. Its name is derived from the Latin *corneolus* meaning "cherry." The Egyptians carried it about their person as a source of energy and for the constant renewal of vitality. In ancient Egypt it was placed in tombs as a "magic armor" for life after death (a custom described in the *Egyptian Book of the Dead*). Hildegard von Bingen sang its praises in the Middle Ages.

Healing properties

By applying carnelian, one can promote good digestion. For lower abdominal pain in women (cysts) and in pregnancy, it should be placed on the pubic bone for twenty minutes every day. It encourages the formation of new blood cells, and bleeding responds favorably to treatment with carnelian. Bleeding gums also benefit

Carnelian is a quartz, which is one of the most common crystal structures

from regular rinsing with carnelian water. Drinking carnelian water helps firm the skin by stimulating the circulation. Psychologically, carnelian increases vitality and zest for life while enhancing stability and the courage to carry out daily tasks.

Magical properties
Red carnelian symbolizes activity. It promotes helpfulness and idealism and encourages community spirit.

Chakra classification
Carnelian works mainly on the sacral chakra.

Star sign
Carnelian is particularly effective for Taurus but it also promotes zest for life in those born under Aries, Gemini and Virgo.

Application and care
Carnelian must be cleansed once a month under warm running water and recharged for quite a long period in the sun. Wear it so that it is in direct contact with the skin. Carnelian water is made by leaving the stone in a glass of water overnight.

Several star signs benefit from the energizing force of carnelian.

Where found	Brazil, Uruguay, India, USA, South Africa, Australia
Color(s)	yellow, orange, red, brown, and all colors in between
Chemical composition	SiO_2 + (Fe, O, OH)
Hardness	6.5 to 7
Available forms	rough stone, tumbled stone, touchstone, necklace, pendant, sphere
Crystallization	it is a kind of quartz, with a trigonal crystallized structure; traces of iron give carnelian its blood red color; it is a member of the chalcedony family

The orange to dark red transparent carnelian owes its color to the presence of iron in the stone. That is why it is so effective in the treatment of blood disorders and blocked arteries.

Celestite

History and legend
Celestite derives its name from the Latin *caelestis*, which means "heavenly," because of its sky-blue color. In ancient Greece it was believed that the stone only worked if it had been given to its owner by a friend or relative. It would then protect the body from all kinds of evil.

The ancient Romans were also familiar with the healing properties of celestite, its calming, fortifying influence on the mind and its ability to drive evil out of a person.

Healing properties

Celestite is a mineral in its own right which is often confused with quartz.

The stone encourages the healing of wounds and regulates the monthly bleeding in women. It is also effective in alleviating pain caused by tension. By relieving anxiety it is also helpful in solving problems of insomnia.

Magical properties
Celestite symbolizes the easing of tension and equilibrium. It works to calm its possessor.

Chakra classification
It works well on the throat chakra.

Star sign
Celestite is connected to both Capricorn and Gemini.

Application and care
Celestite should be cleansed in a bowl filled with tumbled hematites. The points must be positioned so that they always point towards the sky. It only needs recharging occasionally, and this should be done briefly in the sun.

Darker blue celestite is more valuable than the pale blue variety.

Where found	Sicily, Morocco, Madagascar, Egypt; it has become very rare
Color(s)	white to blue, translucent
Chemical composition	$SrSO_4$
Hardness	3 to 3.5
Available forms	the stone has become exceptionally rare ; it is commercially available as a rough stone, geode, crystal
Crystallization	orthorhombic crystal

Because the sites where blue celestite is found have been almost exhausted, rock crystal is vapor-blasted with gold and offered as a mineral called Aqua-Aura. The effect and sparkle are similar to those of celestite but less strong.

Chalcedony

History and legend

The name may come from the city of Chalcedon on the Bosphorus where it was first discovered. Chalcedony was very popular as a decorative stone in antiquity when it was carved with motifs of the air and water gods and goddesses and water sprites. This was because chalcedony was associated with the weather and helped deal with disorders caused by it. The Greek orator Demosthenes (384–322 B.C.) is said to have placed a piece of chalcedony in his mouth when he stood on the shore of the Aegean to practice speaking clearly against the roar of the sea. In Tibet it symbolizes the purity of the Lotus flower and the internalization of the essential.

Since antiquity chalcedony has been the stone of orators.

Healing properties

It is the best stone to use for problems with the neck, tonsils, and vocal cords. It protects against feverish infections and all types of

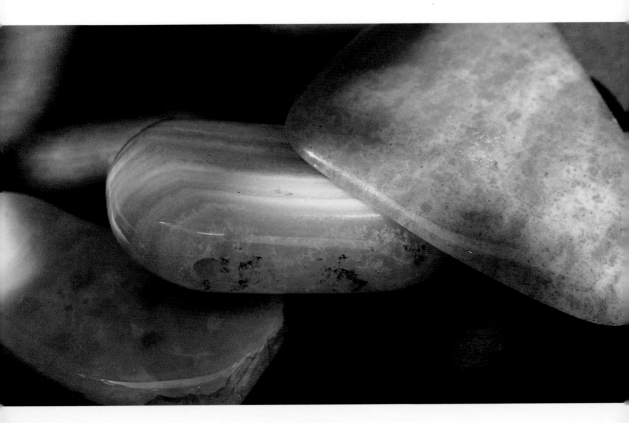

inflammation. Chalcedony water can be made by boiling it with a pinch of salt and is used as a treatment for hoarseness. Psychologically, it offer self-confidence and protection from nightmares.

Magical properties
It symbolizes calmness and composure. For the Tibetans it is the stone of purity and concentration on the essential.

Chakra classification
Chalcedony should be used with the throat chakra, but under no account should the stone be placed with azurite because together the stones would develop too strong a power.

Star sign
Good luck stone for Cancer and protective stone for Sagittarius.

Application and care
Chalcedony should be cleansed once a month under warm running water and, if possible, recharged by being placed overnight in an amethyst geode. An elixir can be made by putting rock crystal and chalcedony in a glass of water and leaving it overnight.

The most beautiful brilliant chalcedony is found in Namibia.

Where found	Namibia, quarries almost exhausted; Brazil, Uruguay, India, Madagascar, USA
Color(s)	almost white to light blue and grayish-blue, often banded with stripes; it is also found as pink, red and copper colored
Chemical composition	SiO_2 + (Fe, Mn, MnO_2, Cu)
Hardness	7
Available forms	rough stone, tumbled stone, touchstone, pendant, necklace
Crystallization	quartz oxide as trigonal crystals in fibrous aggregates

Chalcedony is also called "milk-stone" because it encourages the production of milk in young mothers and prevents breast infections.

Chaorite

History and legend

This stone became known in the West only recently, in 1976, and was named after the place where it was found, the Chaorite river in Siberia. Chaorite can be further divided into small groups because it is made up of many different minerals and metals.

The Mongols use the stone to make decorative objects. On special feast days they boil the stone in tea. This tea is then drunk by all the members of the family in order to strengthen family ties and protect all its members from evil.

Healing properties

Chaorite has only recently been discovered.

Chaorite gives the wearer courage to start afresh. In addition, it strengthens his self-confidence and thirst for action while encouraging orderly habits. It has a positive effect on anxious people. But it has other physical properties: it absorbs ultra-violet and

X-rays so that it protects the skin. In addition, it strengthens the immune system and drives away feelings of insecurity.

Chakra classification
Chaorite is particularly effective on the sixth chakra and should be placed on the forehead.

Star sign
Distinguished by a light-colored striped structure, this stone is not linked to any particularly sign.

Application and care
After every use chaorite must be cleansed under running lukewarm water and then recharged in the sun.

Doctors and nurses working with X-rays should wear chaorite to protect themselves from radiation.

Where found	in only one place, in eastern Siberia
Color(s)	mauve-violet with layered structure, opaque
Chemical composition	Concentration of many metals and minerals
Hardness	6
Available forms	chaorite is a very rare stone; rough stone, tumbled stone, touchstone, necklace
Crystallization	triclinic crystal

The opaque violet chaorite is often confused with the fairly similar sugilite. The characteristic light-colored inclusions are the main difference between the stones.

Chrysoberyl

History and legend

The cat's eye chrysoberyl is particularly sought after because since time immemorial it has been recognized as a stone that protects against the evil eye and black magic. The name was first mentioned by Pliny the Elder who named the stone *chrysos*, the Greek word for gold, because of its yellowish color. It has mainly been used as a gemstone, and was very popular in Victorian times. However, it is now increasingly used as a healing stone. It is easily confused with brazilianite.

Healing properties

It sharpens the sight, protects the visual center in the brain, and combats squints and all kinds of eye inflammations. Cat's eyes are said even to counteract blindness.

The cat's eye is most effective when cut as a cabochon.

The healing power of the chrysoberyl is further enhanced by its

cat's eye shape. A chrysoberyl pendant has a positive effect on the possessor's nervous system. The stone takes away all his negative thoughts, making him far-sighted and able to see more clearly, while making him gentler, kinder, and more tolerant. It also increases optimism. Placed near the bed at night, it drives away nightmares.

Magical properties
Chrysoberyl symbolizes goodness and promotes tolerance and harmony. It also has a positive effect on relationships.

Chakra classification
The chrysoberyl opens up the solar plexus and heart chakras.

Star sign
Chrysoberyl is the stone of Leo.

Application and care
Chrysoberyl must be worn a lot, but without direct contact with the skin. After use as a healing stone, cleanse it immediately under running water. Recharge for only half an hour in the sun.

Chrysoberyl promotes self-knowledge and tolerance.

The chrysoberyl is often mistakenly included in the beryl family. However, it is a mineral in is own right as the German geologist A. G. Werner demonstrated in 1800.

Where found	Brazil, Sri Lanka, Madagascar
Color(s)	golden to yellow-green
Chemical composition	Al_2BeO_4 + Cr, Ti
Hardness	8.5
Available forms	rough crystal, pendant; rarely as a tumbled stone
Crystallization	Copper silicate with an orthorhombic crystal structure, crystallizing as transparent; when chromium is contained in the crystal, it is known as alexandrite

Chrysocolla

History and legend

For thousands of years chrysocolla has been the stone of conciliation and reassurance throughout the world. The ancient Egyptians called it a wise stone because those who wore it came up with clever compromises while also being protected from psychological damage. It was said to make violent-tempered people sensitive and tolerant. This is apparently why Cleopatra carried a chrysocolla with her wherever she went.

Healing properties

For the Egyptians, chrysocolla was the softer brother of the turquoise.

Placed on the forehead it has a cooling effect while also lowering fever. Minor burns are treated by placing a stone on the burn in order to prevent the formation of a blister. Chrysocolla water, sipped slowly, is said to be very refreshing in the case of throat inflammation. It also calms over-excited nerves. It is recommended

that small children wear a chrysocolla pendant directly on the skin to encourage good bone formation and growth. This soft stone has a very beneficial effect on children. It also has positive psychological properties. It lowers stress and tension while reducing anger and hatred.

Magical properties
Chrysocolla symbolizes psychological and mental conciliation. It promotes calmness, goodness and tolerance and strengthens intuition.

Star sign
Chrysocolla associated with Taurus, Cancer, Aquarius, and Libra.

Application and care
Chrysocolla is particularly effective when carried as a touchstone. It should be cleansed once a month under warm running water and then charged overnight in a bowl with tumbled hematite stones.

Chrysocolla is only rarely found today, which is why it is fairly expensive.

In antiquity chrysocolla, a copper mineral, was recognized as a stone of hope by people all over the world.

Where found	Chile, USA, former Soviet Union, South Africa and Israel
Color(s)	turquoise blue to green
Chemical composition	$CuSiO_3 \cdot 2H_2O$ + Al, Fe, P
Hardness	2 to 4, depending on where it is found
Available forms	rough stone, tumbled stone, touchstone, necklace, pyramid, sphere
Crystallization	it is formed as an opaque copper silicate, mainly in seams of copper mines where it is oxidized in water; it is also known as copper pebbles or copper malachite

Chrysoprase

History and legend

The Greeks gave this stone the name chrysoprase, "golden bloom," because of the golden drops that appear to be contained in the stone. It was one of the most valuable and sought-after stones of the Middle Ages. Being a magic stone it was recharged in the open at half moon in order to ensure good health and a happy marriage. Because substantial deposits of the stone were mined in Silesia in the fourteenth century large amounts of precious chrysoprase were used for the now famous decorations of the chapel of St Wenceslas in Prague.

Healing properties

The translucent green to apple-green colored stone is a stone of the heart.

Chrysoprase has a calming influence on the tired, sick heart and creates a harmonious effect on both body and mind. It combats high blood pressure and hardening of the arteries. It also has a positive influence on glandular weaknesses and disorders.

Magical properties

Chrysoprase symbolizes clarity of thought. It leads people to new intellectual approaches and calms them down.

Chakra classification

Chrysoprase has a calming, relaxing effect on the heart chakra, creating internal harmony and contentment.

Star sign

It is an important stone for those born under the sign of Cancer for whom it provides a balance between the unconscious and the conscious.

Application and care

The stone must be worn or laid on for a long time when used for healing purposes. It must be cleansed briefly under running water before each use and recharged overnight among rock crystals every two weeks.

The Australian chrysoprase is one of the most precious gemstones.

Where found	Australia, Brazil, India, South Africa; also in Upper Silesia
Color(s)	apple green and translucent, also almost completely clear
Chemical composition	SiO_2 + (Ni)
Hardness	6.5 to 7
Available forms	rough stone, tumbled stone, touchstone, pendant, necklace, sphere
Crystallization	it is a microcrystalline quartz of the chalcedony family, the color being formed by hydrated silicates; it develops in weathered deposits in seams; trigonal crystal

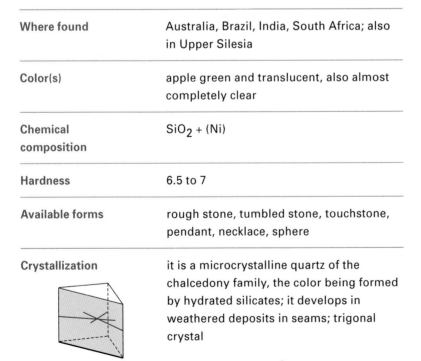

The magnificent green color of chrysoprase is formed by hydrated silicates or nickel oxide. It was Frederick the Great's favorite stone and is one of the most precious representatives of the quartz family.

Cinnabar

History and legend
As early as 700 B.C. the Greeks had established in the mines of Almadén, Spain, to obtain cinnabar ore from which they derived the poisonous quicksilver (mercury). But primitive peoples had also observed the healing power of cinnabar.

Healing powers
Cinnabar transfers its healing qualities to the blood. It can activate the formation of white corpuscles and detoxify and purge the body. It has a positive effect on the immune system, increases resistance to pathogens and helps to avoid infections. Cinnabar placed on the ear helps diminish hearing problems. In addition, it fends off depressing thoughts, dejection and even depression. It frees the wearer from mental problems that might threaten to exhaust him or slow him down emotionally and mentally.

The scientific name for cinnabar is mercury sulfide.

Magical properties

Cinnabar contains negative as well as positive components. On the one hand it is the source of the poisonous metal, mercury, while on the other it possesses various healing powers.

Chakra classification

It has an intense healing power on the root chakra.

Star signs

Not associated with any particular star sign.

Application and use

Cinnabar should be cleansed once a month under warm running water and afterwards recharged again for a short time in the sun. Cinnabar must on no account be taken internally as a tea or elixir!

The color vermilion is obtained from cinnabar.

Where found	mainly in Spain, also in the former Soviet Union, Algeria, USA
Color(s)	red
Chemical composition	HgS
Hardness	2 to 2.5
Available forms	cinnabar is normally available only as a rough crystal
Crystallization	a combination of mercury and sulfur; usually found not as crystals but as mercury ore; trigonal crystal

Cinnabar occurs only rarely in crystalline form. It is usually found in coarse pieces as mercury ore.

Citrine

History and legend

The name citrine is derived from the Latin word *citrus*, meaning "lemon." Until the Middle Ages this name was used to designate a wide range of yellow stones. Citrine has been highly regarded as gemstone and healing stone for almost six thousand years. The soldiers in Caesar's legions wore citrine on their chest because the stone was believed to have life-saving properties in battle. As befits its color, it is recognized as the stone of light, sun, and life.

Healing properties

The purer and more intense the color, the greater the stone's healing properties.

The stone corresponds to the solar plexus and those parts of the body directly connected to it. It has a beneficial influence on the nervous system and is especially good for school children who suffer from lack of concentration. It also combats stress and depression and stimulates the metabolic processes of the liver, stomach,

duodenum, and pancreas. Citrine has a detoxifying effect and a positive influence on the metabolism. It also strengthens the immune system.

Magical properties
Citrine symbolizes individuality and confidence. It brings self-confidence and renewed determination.

Chakra classification
Use on the solar plexus and root chakras. Never combine it with rock crystal! This could create a sun-like energy that could cause burns.

Star sign
Citrine is linked to Gemini and Virgo.

Application and care
Citrine should be cleansed under warm water immediately after use. To achieve the best effect it should be placed directly on the skin.

The yellowish color of citrine is caused by inclusions of manganese and titanium.

The yellow amethyst and smoky quartz can be heated to artificially create citrine.

Where found	Brazil, USA, former Soviet Union, Madagascar, Spain and France
Color(s)	lemon yellow to golden brown, transparent; it is created artificially by heating amethyst or smoky quartz; such stones should be called gold topaz or Madeira topaz
Chemical composition	SiO_2 + (Al, Ca, Fe, Li, Mg, Na)
Hardness	7
Available forms	rough stone, crystal, tumbled stone, touchstone, pendant, sphere, pyramid
Crystalli-zation	a quartz oxide, formed as a hexagonal crystal in granite; the true citrine gains its color from traces of iron; trigonal crystal

Copper

History and legend

For millennia copper has been one of the most important and most useful metals to mankind. In fact it would be hard to imagine an industrialized society without it. Copper is a relatively soft metal (hardness 2.5 to 3), it is easy to solder, and it is very flexible and tough. In addition, it has a very good conductivity that is only slightly less than that of silver. Copper was probably the first metal used to make weapons and objects. Its use to make arrow and spear tips, axes and other tools can be traced back to the fourth millennium (in the Middle East). Its healing properties have been known since the Middle Ages.

The healing power of copper has been used since the Middle Ages.

Healing properties

Copper is used to alleviate the cramp-like pains of menstruation. It is also said to promote the smooth functioning of the glands. In

addition, it can prevent wear and tear and calcification of the joints. Psychologically, copper encourages a positive attitude and self-confidence. As a result, it improves decision making and brings harmony among the members of a family.

Chakra classification
Copper can be used effectively on all chakras but is particularly effective on the heart and root chakras as preparation for meditation.

Star sign
Not associated with any particular star sign.

Application and care
Copper should cleansed by being placed overnight in a bowl filled with tumbled hematite stones. It must not come into contact with water, which is why one should never drink copper water. For recharging, it should simply be placed in the sun. Wear copper directly on the skin, place it under the pillow or carry it in your pocket.

Copper is an orange-colored metal.

Copper is best able to develop its healing powers when worn directly on the skin, in the form of a bracelet or necklace.

Where found	all over the world; common in deposits in the USA (Michigan)
Color(s)	orange, copper red
Chemical composition	Cu
Hardness	2.5 to 3
Available forms	nugget, touchstone, pendant, amulets
Crystallization	cubic, usually twisted crystal form; idiomorphic structure

Coral

History and legend
The ancient Egyptians placed pieces of coral in tombs as a protection against evil spirits because they believed that each piece contained a drop of divine blood. According to Greek mythology, when Perseus chopped off the head of the Gorgon Medusa, some drops of blood splashed into the sea and there solidified into coral. The ancient Iranian prophet and founder of their religion, Zoroaster, perceived coral as a magical protective stone against diseases and magic, a conclusion that was later supported by Paracelsus (1494–1541).

Healing properties

Since time immemorial coral has been considered a magical "stone."

Basically, coral protects against negative energy while also preventing loss of energy. That is why coral jewelry is recommended for menopausal women. Similarly it can prevent osteoporosis and also promotes healthy bone formation in children. Growth

and formation of new tissue of every kind are also promoted by coral. In accordance with its red color, coral is also beneficial in the treatment of blood and circulation disorders. Psychologically, it strengthens love and the need for partnership and makes the wearer immune to envy and resentment.

Magical properties
Coral symbolizes joy and happiness. It enables the wearer to enjoy life. According to legend it consists of divine blood.

Chakra classification
Red coral should be used on the root chakra, black coral on the solar plexus. and pink coral on the heart chakra.

Star sign
Red coral is associated with Scorpio, black coral with Capricorn, pink coral with Taurus.

Application and care
Because there are many fakes, it is important to trust the person you are buying from. Coral is cleansed by being left overnight in salt water once a month. It can also be placed dry in sea salt.

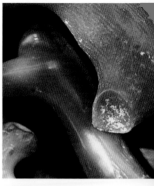

Coral is a very powerful healing stone that has many uses.

Where found	reefs in warm seas, particularly east of Australia (beautifully colored coral), around Japan, Africa, Mediterranean and Canary Islands
Color(s)	pink, salmon pink, red, also white and black
Chemical composition	organic substances + $CaCO_3$
Hardness	3 to 4
Available forms	as a jewel and as large pieces for display in rooms
Crystallization	amorphous stone

Coral is not a mineral but the skeleton of sea creatures, thus organic in origin. Developed over many thousands of years, it consists almost entirely of calcium.

Diamond

History and legend

Diamonds, especially the celebrated brilliant-cut stones, are surrounded by stories of fame and grandeur, murder and misfortune. Pliny the Elder called it the king of all stones "the most precious of all human possessions ...long known only to kings and then only to a few." In the Middle Ages people spoke of the "divine brilliance on earth" when describing its sparkle, a reference to its very high refractive index. In India the diamond, the "invincible stone," was considered the stone of virtue and justice. The ruler administered justice while holding a diamond.

The name "diamond" is of Latin origin (adamas = invincible).

Because it is the hardest of all stones it has become an indispensable tool in many areas of industrial production. Diamond mining for this purpose is therefore of the greatest economic and political importance. By comparison the significance of diamonds in jewelry fades into the background.

Healing properties

A small piece of rough diamond placed overnight in a glass of water to be drunk the following morning is an excellent fortifying remedy for combating stress, during convalescence and periods of exhaustion. It also removes blockages and impurities. Placed as a "third eye" between the eyebrows, a diamond will help combat mental illness. Diamond encourages self-confidence and a desire for independence while counteracting jealousy.

Magical properties

The diamond symbolizes wisdom and enlightenment, purity and clarity. It provides protection, preserves peace and gives power.

Chakra classification

The diamond has a harmonizing influence on all the chakras.

Star sign

It is the lucky stone of Leo.

Application and care

Diamonds should not be cleansed or charged.

A diamond has greater healing power when it is cut as a brilliant.

Where found	Kimberley (Africa), Brazil, Australia, Siberia
Color(s)	white to yellowish and brownish, transparent
Chemical composition	C + (Al, Ca, Fe)
Hardness	10, the hardest of all stones
Available forms	rough diamond, cut jewel
Crystallization	Diamonds are pure carbon that was formed in old volcanoes under very high pressure at a temperature of about 1,300 °C when it forms cubes and octahedrons.

The brilliant cut was first executed by Louis van Berquen in 1456. A brilliant-cut diamond is the most expensive of all gemstones and the one in greatest demand.

Diopside

History and legend

The name of the stone comes from the Greek *dis* meaning "double," *opsis* meaning "sight," and *idos* meaning "shape." Diopside was known as a gemstone in antiquity. The Greeks believed that star diopsides, diopsides with a star shape on the surface, were small sparkling stars that had fallen from the sky and turned into stones as a result. They retained their starry sparkle as a reminder of their previous existence in the sky.

Healing properties

Green diopside is found mainly in Austria and Brazil.

There are several varieties of diopside. There are black, green, and blue varieties as well as the star diopside. Green diopside is particularly recommended for kidney and bladder problems. The other stones are beneficial in the treatment of deficiencies and clotting of the blood.

Psychologically, diopside encourages a positive attitude to life and ensures a well-balanced temperament. It can help its possessor solve problems that have burdened him for years.

Chakra classification
Diopside is most effective when used on the heart chakra.

Star sign
Not associated with any particular star sign.

Application and care
Diopside should be cleansed once a month under warm running water. Diopside necklaces should be cleansed by being placed in a bowl of tumbled hematite stones. Diopsides are very rich in energy and after cleansing they should be recharged for a few hours in the hottest midday sun.

Green diopside is used in the treatment of kidney and bladder problems.

People who easily bruise should always wear or carry a necklace of black diopside or star diopside. The stones harmonize the clotting factor in the blood.

Where found	India, Madagascar, Sri Lanka; the green stones are found in Austria and Brazil
Color(s)	green, bluish, black, with star shape
Chemical composition	$CaMg [Si_2O_6]$
Hardness	5 to 6
Available forms	crystals, crystal pieces, also as tumbled stones
Crystallization	monoclinic crystal

Dioptase

History and legend

It was only in the eighteenth century, in 1797, that dioptase was recognized as a copper mineral and thus distinguished from emerald. Because of its green color it was called "copper emerald" for a long time. The name is derived from the Greek *diopteia* meaning "transparent." As a highly sought-after gemstone, it was considered the guardian of prosperity and beauty as well as the stone of Venus.

Healing properties

Dioptase has direct and indirect effects on the heart; it works by calming and strengthening it. Combined with pink kunzite, it heightens its possessor's sensitivity. It is used in treating the liver and gall bladder because of its pain relieving and antispasmodic properties. It is also used to alleviate headaches. Psychologically it makes its possessor more sensitive and open to nature and the environment.

The transparent dark green dioptase is one of the most sought-after minerals.

Magical properties
Dioptase symbolizes wealth and abundance. According to legend it is the precious stone that represents prosperity and beauty.

Chakra classification
It is particularly effective on the heart chakra. Because it only comes in the form of very small crystals, dioptase should be placed very carefully on the appropriate place, namely in the middle of the chest, for half an hour. The person treated should be completely relaxed as he lies on his back and concentrate all his thoughts on the heart center.

Star sign
Not associated with any particular star sign.

Application and care
Dioptase should not be cleansed in water but should be placed once a month among dry tumbled hematite stones. When not in use, dioptase is best stored with pink kunzite and rock crystal.

Until the end of the eighteenth century dioptase was thought to be a type of emerald.

Dioptase is said to remedy diseases of the primary and secondary sexual organs. It also increases sexual potency and libido.

Where found	South-West Africa, Zaire, USA (Arizona) and also the former Soviet Union
Color(s)	dark green, transparent
Chemical composition	$Cu_6 [Si_6O_{18}] \cdot 6\,H_2O$
Hardness	5
Available forms	the stone is very rare; prepared gemstones
Crystallization	Dioptase is a trigonal crystallized combination of copper and silica, that forms only groups of small crystals; it is found in limestone and sandstone seams in copper mining areas; trigonal or hexagonal crystal

Dolomite

History and legend
In the Middle Ages physicians and alchemists ground the stone dolomite into powder and used it as a treatment for skin rashes and bone diseases. It was named after the French mineralogist D. Gratet de Dolomieu who first described the mineral in 1791.

Healing properties
Dolomite is used to treat skin rashes and bone diseases. It is particularly therapeutic in the form of healing water, which is dabbed on the infected spot or fungal infection. Dolomite neutralizes excess acid which is why it is effective in alleviating stomach and intestinal disorders. It is used to soften hardened scar tissue and smooth unsightly scarring. It regulates metabolic processes and reduces food and pollen allergies. Sugar dolomite is particularly effective in protecting the skin from diseases and dryness. It also

There are white, brown, yellowish, and transparent dolomites.

has strong detoxifying properties that help prevent hardening of the arteries and high cholesterol. In addition, it protects the pancreas, thyroid gland, ovaries, and testicles against disease.

Chakra classification
Placed on the forehead, belly button, or between the breasts, it has harmonizing effect and protects from low self-esteem.

Star sign
Not associated with any particular star sign.

Application and care
Dolomite can be cleansed under warm running water. More effective is a monthly cleansing overnight in a bowl of tumbled hematite stones.

Sugar dolomite is a white dolomite with gold-colored inclusions of pyrites.

Where found	Switzerland, Austria, Yugoslavia, Germany; particularly in the Dolomites
Color(s)	brown to red with dark layers; also white, yellowish to transparent; sugar dolomite is white dolomite with gold-colored inclusions of pyrites
Chemical composition	$CaMg(CO_3)_2$ + Fe, Mn; $CaMg(CO_3)_2$
Hardness	5 to 6
Available forms	rough stone, crystal, tumbled stone, touchstone, pendant, sphere
Crystallization	typical crystals are orthorhombic with a poor surface, shaped into "saddle" and "inlaid" forms; crystals with a rich surface are particularly rare

Dolomite is mined to obtain magnesium salts that are used in industry and medicine. There are spectacular formations of this rock in the mountain region of the Dolomites.

Dumortierite

History and legend

Dumortierite was discovered about a hundred years ago by a French paleontologist named Dumortier. Africans had long believed that the stone was petrified water, because it was always found in the vicinity of water. The stone is a mineral-rich aluminum silicate. Its various shades of blue, which range from dark to violet blue, are caused by the presence of manganese, iron, and zinc.

Healing properties

This stone can relieve stomach trouble, vomiting, and nausea. After long exposure to the sun, it is helpful in the treatment of skin irritation and also headaches.

Dumortierite calms the nerves and alleviates stress-induced pain such as tension and headaches.

Dumortierite is frequently found in regions abounding in watercourses.

Magical properties
Dumortierite symbolizes partnership and encourages tolerance towards other people.

Chakra classification
Placed on the throat chakra during meditation it produces a feeling of deep relaxation and equilibrium. Lie completely relaxed on your back and place the stone on your throat. This will gently stimulate and harmonize the throat chakra.

Star sign
Dumortierite is linked to Sagittarius.

Application and care
The stone should be rinsed once a week under warm running water and recharged by placing it among lead crystals for a period of two hours.

The stone's blue color is caused by the presence of manganese, iron and zinc.

Where found	Madagascar, Canada, USA, Namibia; particularly in South Africa
Color(s)	blue, in many shades extending to violet-blue
Chemical composition	$(Al, Fe)_7 [O_3/BO_3/(SiO_4)_3] + Mn$
Hardness	7
Available forms	chiefly found as a tumbled stone and gemstone
Crystallization	it is an aluminum silicate mineral with traces of manganese, iron, and zinc giving it its blue color; orthorhombic crystal

Dumortierite makes troublesome everyday tasks more bearable. It induces deep relaxation and a feeling of harmony and calm.

Emerald

History and legend

In ancient mythology emerald was associated with Mercury, the messenger of the gods and god of travel; it therefore follows that it is the protection stone of travelers. Emeralds from the vicinity of the Red Sea were the foundation of the wealth of the Pharaohs. Cleopatra sought to achieve eternal youth and beauty through the reflection of the most precious emeralds on her skin.

The New World provided Europe with a rich source of emeralds. Many of the most famous emeralds were stolen from the Incas by the conquistadors.

The emerald has been valued by all cultures and ruling houses in every period.

Healing powers

Pliny the Elder wrote: "When the eyes are weakened, they are strengthened again by observing the emerald; the stone's mild green expels the weariness." Today fragments of emerald are still

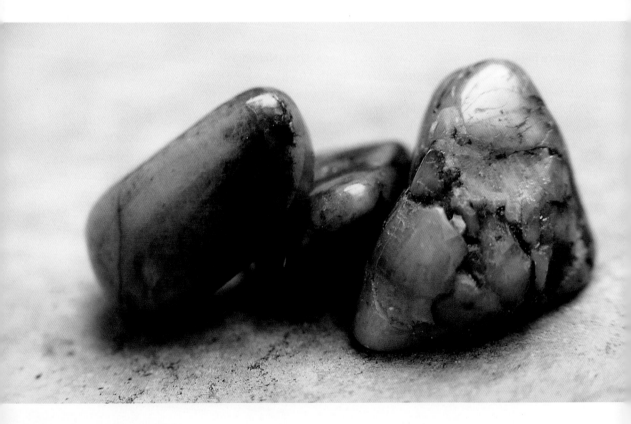

put in the corner of the eye to stabilize the vision. An emerald can also be effective against headaches. It promotes mental growth, farsightedness and perceptiveness. With it misfortunes can be better managed.

Magical properties

The green emerald symbolizes hope and development. It stands for maturity and was a stone of divine intuition for the Greeks.

Chakra classification

The energy of the emerald flows best over the heart chakra.

Star sign

The emerald is assigned to Cancer.

Application and care

After each application, the stone should be regularly cleansed under running water. Once a month it should be recharged in the sun. It develops its strength particularly in association with rock crystal and ruby.

The emerald promotes harmony and balance.

Where found	Columbia, Urals, Rhodesia, Australia, Brazil, India, and Pakistan
Color(s)	various depths of green
Chemical composition	$Al_2Be_3 (Si_6O_{18})$ + K, Li, Na + (Cr)
Hardness	7 to 8
Available forms	gem essence, small fragments for laying on the body or worn as a necklace; cut as precious jewelry
Crystallization	part of the beryl family, forming hexagonal crystals; the green color comes from traces of chromium

The emerald is regarded as a powerful stone for all problems of impaired balance; it is used for multiple sclerosis, Parkinson's disease, epilepsy and various kinds of vertigo.

Epidote

History and legend
The stone takes it name from the Greek *epidosis*, meaning "grow-ing together." It consists of a combination of deformed red jasper and green epidote solidly bound together. From this it conveys the meaning that what comes together, belongs together.

Healing powers
Epidote strengthens the body's condition and immune system. It can be used for all illnesses because of this strengthening effect; it also decreases the respective physical weakness. In addition it is useful for stimulating the digestion and metabolism. It helps things that are lost to be found again. It is good for recuperating after weakness caused by serious illnesses. It relaxes the abdom-inal area and relieves phlegm in the respiratory tract. Epidote encourages patience, develops the psyche and gives optimism and

Epidote is known for its beneficial effect on equilibrium.

self-confidence. Sorrow cannot harm the person carrying it, nor will he be affected by despair or self-pity.

Magical properties
The one who carries epidote will find things that have been lost.

Chakra classification
It affects the heart chakra and the secondary chakras of the hand.

Star sign
The stone is assigned to the star sign Gemini as well as Libra.

Application and care
Healing stones should be cleansed under running water, while larger pieces are better dried under tumbled hematite stones. Once a month they should be recharged for several hours in a group of rock crystals.

Epidote is a reddish stone with green fields.

Where found	South Africa, Brazil, China
Color(s)	reddish with green specks or the reverse
Chemical composition	$Ca_2 (Al, Fe) Al_2 [O/OH/SiO_4/Si_2O_7]$ + K, Mg, Mn, Sr, Ti
Hardness	6 to 7
Available forms	tumbled stones, necklaces and pendants are widely found
Crystallization	mixture of calcium, iron and aluminum, rich in minerals; monoclinic crystal

Epidote had particularly good effects on the lower genital areas of men and women, easing and relaxing them.

Falcon's eye

History and legend

When the stone known as falcon's eye is cut into a round shape, its fibrous deposits are reminiscent of an eye. This led to the belief that worn as an amulet it protected its possessor against the evil eye, witches and demons. In Arab culture, the falcon's eye is believed to promote cheerfulness in the wearer.

Healing properties

The bluish falcon's eye with silvery luster is a member of the quartz family.

Short-sightedness, eye infections and eye disorders of all kinds can be treated with a falcon's eye. The stone is cut into slices and these pieces are heated in warm water, then placed on the eyelids. Falcon's eye also alleviates headaches and migraines. As in the case of many other stones, it may be assumed that the appearance and name of this stone have strongly influenced its healing applications. The stone is said to promote single-

mindedness in its possessor, helping him to recognize his own weaknesses.

Magical properties
The falcon's eye symbolizes attentiveness; its wearer begins to view the world and his fellow-creatures with affection.

Chakra classification
Place the falcon's eye on the forehead chakra.

Star sign
The falcon's eye is linked to Aquarius.

Application and care
The falcon's eye blocks the flow of energy, which is why it should never be worn for more than three days in a row. It should not be cleansed in water but in dry tumbled hematite stones. It is then recharged among rock crystals.

In order to be an effective protection, the falcon's eye must be worn visibly.

Where found	South Africa and Western Australia, India and USA
Color(s)	blue-green to blue-gray and blue-black
Chemical composition	$SiO_2 + Na_2 (La, Fe, Mg)_5 [OH/Si_4O_{11}]_2 + P$
Hardness	7
Available forms	polished for hand and pocket and for laying on the body; as a gemstone
Crystallization	falcon's eye is a quartz aggregate whose gleam is provided by sparkling inclusions of fibrous hornblende and blue-black asbestos fibers that are solidly enclosed within the quartz; trigonal crystal

At the time when witches were persecuted, a falcon's eye was put in front of the eyes of women who were suspected of being witches. If they averted their gaze, they were deemed guilty.

Fire opal

History and legend

Historically the fire opal has been considered to be the stone of fervent love and strength. As the stone is linked to the planet Mars, it is a talisman for explorers and conquerors, who believe it will ensure the success of their expeditions and help them overcome danger. The color of fire opal is its most beautiful and strongest characteristic. The colors range from orange shades to transparent red. The more valuable pieces have a shimmering play of colors. The Persians and Indians believed that because of the clarity and intensity of the colors the fire opal could only have originated in the waters of Paradise.

Fire opals are highly sought after as gemstones with powerful healing properties.

During his first great journey to South and Central America, Alexander von Humboldt (1769–1859) brought back the first fire opal from Mexico in 1804. Fire opals were used by the Aztecs and Mayas as gemstones, in mosaics and for ritual purposes.

Healing properties

The fire opal stimulates sexuality. It also strengthens the immune system and stabilizes the circulation of the blood. It increases the wearer's energy and helps in combating aboulia (a lack of resolution). On a psychic level it also produces positive vibrations. The fire opal brings movement into life by encouraging enthusiasm and spontaneity, it raises energy levels and counteracts over-intellectualization. It is believed that when someone offers a fire opal to a person they desire very much, the object of affection will soon become devoted to the giver.

Chakra classification

Use the fire opal on the root chakra. In order to do this you should lie on your stomach. Then place the stone on your lower back, preferably directly on the skin.

Star sign

The fire opal is particularly suited to Aries.

Application and care

Keep the fire opal in a glass of water. In this way it will constantly be cleansed and recharged. Leave it alone for some time or it will become cloudy.

The Indians used fire opals to treat heart and circulation problems.

If in a relationship or marriage you notice that the fire opal is turning cloudy, it means that you must make urgent changes. If the stone shows a crack, it means that a change is about to happen.

Where found	Mexico, Australia, Brazil, Denmark, Guatemala, Kazakhstan
Color(s)	brown, reddish-brown, fiery red to orange-yellow; it ranges from transparent to translucent
Chemical composition	$SiO_2 + H_2O$
Hardness	6 to 6.5
Available forms	rough stone, tumbled stone, also worked as a jewel
Crystallization	amorphous stone

Flint

History and legend
In the Stone Age flint was the basic raw material used to make
arrow points, knives, and cutting blades. These were then offered
to the gods in gratitude for successful hunting expeditions. Flint
is easy to work: when it is knocked against a hard surface it will
fracture in what is known as a conchoidal break with sharp-edged
surfaces. Flints produce sparks when they are struck against
each other. The use of flint as a tool was only abandoned when man
learned to forge metal. In Mexico and the United States, the Indians still sell beautiful flint-tipped arrows.

Healing properties
*Flints are
distinguished by
their great hardness.*
Flint stimulates a healthy functioning of the respiratory tract and
lungs. It purifies the blood through the kidneys and strengthens
the nervous system. Nervous disorders are also alleviated with

flint. It can also help in the treatment of ganglions. Flint encourages self-confidence, especially in older people, and enables them to lead more active lives. It also has a beneficial influence on the psyche by promoting self-assurance and encouraging individualism. Placed under the pillow it is said to prevent nightmares.

Chakra classification
Use flint on the root chakra.

Star sign
Not associated with any particular star sign.

Application and care
Flint should be cleansed at least once a month under running warm water. It is then recharged by being placed for two or three hours in the hot midday sun or among rock crystals.

Older people in particular benefit from the invigorating effect of flint.

Where found	England, Scotland, Baltic countries, Egypt, USA, Brazil, Mexico, Australia
Color(s)	gray, black, black and white, beige; it is often patterned
Chemical composition	SiO_2
Hardness	7
Available forms	rough stone, tumbled stone, touchstone, pendant
Crystallization	trigonal crystal

Flints are jasper-like quartz compounds that range in color from black, black and white, gray, beige and white, often with patterns reminiscent of runes.

Fluorite

History and legend

Fluorite belongs to the spar family. Like all other members, fluorite, also known as feldspar, can be separated into flakes. Because of its wide range of colors it is often said that it contains something of all the other gemstones in it. According to folklore, it is the home of rainbows.

Healing properties

The colorful rainbow fluorite combines the healing properties of almost all other healing stones.

It gradually removes pain when placed directly on the affected area. The direct application of the stone is particularly helpful for ailments such as energy blockages, respiratory problems, suppurating wounds and skin diseases as well as arthritis. Fluorite can also be used to ease joint problems and stiffness. In these cases too, the stone should be applied on the site of the problem. Fluorite will also awaken suppressed feelings and combat narrow-mindedness.

Magical properties
Fluorite symbolizes responsibility and obedience.

Chakra classification
The rainbow-colored stones work well on the third eye and the yellow stones work on the solar plexus chakra.

Star sign
Fluorite is linked to Scorpio, Aquarius, and Pisces.

Application and care
Fluorite is cleansed in warm water. After cleansing it should be charged in the sun or among rock crystals.

Fluorite is a very popular stone because of its many crystal shapes and colors.

Where found	Spain, England, USA, Mexico, particularly China
Color(s)	yellow, violet, green as well as rainbow-colored
Chemical composition	CaF_2 + (C, Cl, Ce, Fe, Y)
Hardness	4
Available forms	pieces of feldspar, displayed in rooms, and as a learning and organizational stone; available commercially as a geode, touchstone, necklace, tumbled stone and gemstone
Crystallization	it originates in acidic magnetic rocks, occasionally as a result of weathering processes; cubic crystal

Yellow fluorite helps in the treatment of diseases of the spleen and kidney. Green fluorite relieves asthma and regenerates the lung tissues. Blue fluorite (blue john) combats colds, infections and sudden circulation problems, while violet fluorite has a beneficial effect on the head and brain.

Garnet

History and legend
Since antiquity garnets have been famous for their inner sparkle. The crown of the German emperor Otto (912–973) was decorated with the most famous garnet of all, known as the "Wise One." Knights and warriors decorated their weapons and shields with garnets. Hildegard von Bingen prescribed garnet to strengthen the heart while in Indian mythology garnet is called the "Kundalini fire" (fire of eternal metamorphosis). In Hinduism and Buddhism it is seen as a holy stone that enlightens the soul and gives wisdom.

Healing properties

Garnet is believed to have an energizing effect on one's sex life.

Garnet is said to help in the treatment of disturbed blood circulation and to strengthen the heart. It brings vitality during the catabolic process and strengthens the memory. In passionate people the stone can also release a negative energy.

Magical properties
Garnet symbolizes constructiveness. Mystics believe it brightens dark souls and brings hope to people.

Chakra classification
Garnet works best on the root and sacral chakras.

Star sign
Garnet is particularly good for Aries and Scorpio.

Application and care
Direct contact with the skin is important. When little garnet beads move as part of a necklace, the effect of the stone is multiplied several times. Garnet should cleansed under running hand-hot water every month. Place the garnet in the sun to recharge it.

The otherwise dull-colored mineral only develops its sparkle when cut.

Where found	Bohemia; Madagascar, India, Canada, South Africa, Australia, USA
Color(s)	red and dark red to rust red, as well as yellow, green and black
Chemical composition	ions of two metals $(SiO_4)_3$ + (another metal)
Hardness	7 to 7.5 depending on variety
Available forms	as a rough stone for protection and energy; also used in jewelry
Crystallization	a magnesium-aluminum mineral, that appears in many different varieties, but all with the same structure and almost the same form in crystalline slate or other tertiary rocks; forms transparent to opaque cubic forms

Anyone subject to depression should always carry a tumbled garnet with him. It encourages feelings of joy, willpower and hope, while its fiery color drives away tiredness and stimulates the imagination.

Gold

History and legend

Gold has symbolized power and wealth since time immemorial. Even today, most governments endeavor to have the gold equivalent of the paper currency in their state reserves. Over the millennia the great value attached to gold has been reflected in precious jewelry, amulets, death-masks, figurines, facings, coating of porcelain and even gold threads in fabrics. "Everything is moved by gold, everything depends on gold" Gretchen cries plaintively in Goethe's Faust while the philosopher describes gold as follows: "Gold is the sovereign of all sovereigns" (Karl Weber).

Gold increases the healing properties of all stones.

Healing properties

Because gold increases the healing properties of stones, jewelry with stones set in gold always has a special energy. Psychologically,

gold increases the wearer's self-confidence. This can sometimes lead to arrogance, a negative effect of gold.

Gold symbolizes wealth and power.

Magical properties
This precious metal is associated with love and faithfulness and as such is the epitome of the perfect gift.

Chakra classification
Used on the heart and throat chakras, it encourages people to accept innovation.

Star sign
Not associated with any particular star sign.

Application and care
Healing stones, set in gold, make powerful amulets. Cleanse and discharge once a month under running warm water. Wear frequently in the sun to recharge.

Where found	South Africa, former Soviet Union, Australia; USA
Color(s)	golden yellow
Chemical composition	Au
Hardness	2.5 to 3
Available forms	to harden it and work it better, gold is alloyed: with titanium for white gold, brass for yellow gold and copper for red gold. The ratio of the metals to each other is defined by standards and is hallmarked with a punch on pieces once made.
Crystallization	a soft element, mined in goldfields or obtained from rivers, where nuggets and gold dust are panned; cubic crystal

Until now a total of 75,000 tons of gold have been mined from the earth. As well as being used for jewelry, much of it is stored in bullion vaults and over 200 pounds of gold were found in the tomb of Tutankhamun.

Grossular

History and legend

The very special healing properties of grossular have been known since time immemorial but it is also highly valued as a precious gemstones. The ancient Greeks and Romans believed that it could influence the behavior of the gods. The name is derived from the Latin *ribes grossularia*, which means "gooseberry." The clear, green grossular and the orange-colored hessonite have often been confused with emerald and beryl. They were very popular with the ancient Greeks and Romans because of their beautiful appearance.

Healing properties

Green grossular stones are the most effective.

Grossular (green garnet) is used as a healing stone in the treatment of bones. It can therefore be used to alleviate osteoporosis and it is also used to treat rheumatism and arthritis. The stone is

effective in the treatment of liver and gall bladder problems. In addition, grossular is also highly effective in the treatment of psychosomatic illnesses. For students it removes the fear of exams.

Chakra classification
Grossular is most effective when placed on the the heart chakra.

Star sign
Not associated with any particular star sign.

Application and care
The stone should be discharged and cleansed regularly, at least once a month, by being placed overnight in a bowl filled with tumbled hematite stones. After being discharged it should be recharged by being placed for a few hours among rock crystals or in full sunlight.

The largest and most beautiful grossular stones come from Queensland in Australia.

Where found	occurs throughout the world, the most beautiful are found in Queensland, Australia
Color(s)	brownish-orange, greenish-brown, green
Chemical composition	$Ca_3Al_2[SiO_4]_3$ (hessonite: with Fe)
Hardness	6.5 to 7
Available forms	crystal, tumbled stone, touchstone, also as pendants and cabochons
Crystallization	cubic crystal

The green to green-brown grossular and orange-brown hessonite are members of the garnet family but are relatively rare representatives of this group.

Heliodor

History and legend

The Greeks firmly believed that this stone contained the power and warmth of the sun and that it was responsible for the alternation of day and night. This belief is reflected in the name itself, the Greek *heliodor* meaning "gift of the sun." The stone was then forgotten for a long time and was only recently rediscovered. Significant deposits of heliodor were found at the beginning of the twentieth century in South-West Africa. A few specimens surfaced earlier in Brazil and Madagascar.

Heliodor necklaces, often combined with other stones of the beryl family, have powerful healing properties.

Healing properties

The light green or yellowish-green transparent heliodor has a stimulating effect on the vegetative nervous system and a particularly beneficial effect on the solar plexus. It can counteract the over-reactions and hyperactivity of the body. Heliodor water

eases stiff muscles and cramp. Psychologically, it brings equilibrium to the wearer and gives him courage to live. It promises the wearer charisma and personality. It stimulates the mind and promotes a clear head, especially in negotiations and mentally demanding work.

Chakra classification
Heliodor works well on the navel and heart chakras.

Star sign
Not associated with any particular star sign.

Application and care
Heliodor should be stored overnight in a bowl of dry, tumbled hematite stones. Rub the stone lightly under warm running water to discharge and cleanse.

Heliodor was identified both as a protective stone and a rejuvenating healing stone in pre-Christian times.

Where found	Brazil, USA, Sri Lanka, South Africa
Color(s)	variety of beryl ranging from blue-green to yellow
Chemical composition	$Al_2Be_3 [Si_6O_{18}]$
Hardness	7.5 to 8
Available forms	the heliodor is used as a rough stone and tumbled stone; in its cut form it is worn as jewelry
Crystallization	hexagonal crystal

Heliodor belongs to the beryl family and owes its greenish color to the presence of small amounts of iron and chromium. Like all beryls it is a highly sought after healing stone.

Heliotrope

History and legend

The name is derived from the Greek and means "turning the sun." The ancient Greeks perceived the heliotrope as the connecting stone between the gods, men, and the earth. The Egyptians believed it be a powerful protective stone. Hildegard von Bingen further shrouded it in mystery with the legend that its red "drops" were the blood of Christ. As a result, the heliotrope became the holy protective stone of the crusaders. It is also called bloodstone.

Healing properties

The heliotrope must not be used as a rough stone because it has razor-sharp edges.

The stone is used to combat bladder inflammation, in which case it should be applied for twenty minutes. It is also an excellent stone for the heart, alleviating pain while regulating arrhythmia and disturbed circulation of the coronary vessels. It cleanses and fortifies blood-carrying organs such as the liver, kidneys, lungs and spleen.

Magical properties
The heliotrope symbolizes sympathy and humility. The ancient Greeks saw its green color as the symbol of the earth.

Chakra classification
The heliotrope works best on the heart chakra.

Star sign
Not associated with any particular star sign.

Application and care
The heliotrope must not be used as a rough stone. It should be cleansed under warm running water after each use, then recharged among rock crystals.

When polished, the heliotrope can be used in massage.

Where found	the most beautiful pieces are found in India and China; it is also found in Australia, Brazil and USA
Color(s)	opaque dark green with pink, orange and red spots, stripes or fields
Chemical composition	SiO_2 + Al, Fe, Mg, OH, Si
Hardness	7
Available forms	for holding or wearing; worn rough or polished as jewelry; for display in the room
Crystallization	this chalcedony is basically green in color (as a result of containing plates of chloride), and the red color comes from iron oxide; because of this red color it has been called "bloodstone" but it has nothing to do with either jasper or hematite; trigonal crystal

The heliotrope is reputed to be a good stone for pregnant women. Psychologically it protects against nightmares and promotes concentration during the day.

Hematite

History and legend

The ancient Egyptians used hematite to staunch blood and to promote the formation of blood cells. In the Middle Ages it was known as "blood stone" since the water used for polishing it becomes red during the process. Because of its styptic properties it was often given to warriors going to battle.

Healing properties

All processes connected with the blood benefit from contact with hematite.

As well as staunching blood, hematite promotes the formation of blood cells. It is used to stabilize the circulation of blood and combats venous hyperemia and embolism. Its regenerative power is beneficial for eye problems (place a polished stone on the eyelid) and promotes healthy sleep when placed under the pillow with rose quartz. Caution is required since hematite can lead to inflammations! Psychologically, it encourages spontaneity and zest for life.

Magical properties

Hematite symbolizes courage and was known as "blood stone" in the Middle Ages, staunching blood and promoting the formation of new blood cells.

Chakra classification

Particularly effective on the root chakra.

Star sign

The stone is assigned to Scorpio whom it not only protects but also warns of danger by changing temperature.

Application and care

Never wear hematite near inflammations of any kind; it can exacerbate them. Never discharge in water. Placed among tumbled rock crystals hematite releases negative energy and at the same time becomes recharged with positive energy.

A hematite necklace is best worn directly on the skin.

Where found	USA, Canada, Great Britain, Italy, Switzerland, Sweden and Urals
Color(s)	gray-black, dark reddish-brown, shiny metallic
Chemical composition	Fe_2O_3 + Mg, Ti + (Al, Cr, Mn, Si, H_2O)
Hardness	5.5 to 6.5
Available forms	as a rough stone placed under the pillow; cut and polished as an amulet; worn as a necklace
Crystallization	known as "kidney ore" (from its kidney-like shape), it is usually found crystallized as fibrous or leaf-like crystals in the oxidized parts of iron deposits; it is also often found associated with volcanic lava; iron oxide gives it its black sheen; trigonal crystal

Hematite is said to protect the wearer's vital energy and guarantee survival. Hematite amulets have been found in nearly every pharaoh's tomb as a support in the afterlife.

Herkimer diamond

History and legend

Herkimer diamond has always been a sought-after stone, not least because of its strong energy and healing powers, especially in combination with other healing stones. It takes its name from the site where it is found, Herkimer County in New York State.

Healing properties

Herkimer diamonds are quartz crystals with a diamond-like crystal structure. Herkimer diamond increases the effectiveness of other stones and is therefore used in combination with others, not on its own. The stones can release tension, and they also have far-reaching powers that make them ideal stones for detoxifying the whole body. In addition they strengthen the body's own natural mechanisms. The Herkimer diamond opens up the user's soul to new impressions and gives him a feeling of openness.

Herkimer diamonds are quartz crystals with a diamond-like crystal structure.

Magical properties

Herkimer diamond symbolizes openness: the wearer is open to new impressions and the surrounding world.

Chakra classification

It works particularly well on the heart and solar plexus chakras. It is recommended that Herkimer diamond should be used in combination with other stones in order to increase their effectiveness.

Star sign

Works particularly well for Capricorn and Sagittarius.

Application and care

It should be cleansed once a month under warm running water, then recharged among rock crystals or exposed to the sun for a long time.

Prospecting for these quartz crystals still takes place in the United States today.

Where found	exclusively in New York State
Color(s)	gray-white to translucent
Chemical composition	SiO_2
Hardness	7
Available forms	pieces are very hard to find and extremely expensive; usually they are already faceted; the herkimer diamond is particularly useful in conjunction with other therapeutic stones, because it reinforces their effect
Crystallization	it is a doubled quartz crystal, very similar to diamond but without its hardness and utility for machining other materials; trigonal crystal

These gray-white to transparent quartz crystals are sought after by collectors. As well as being very beautiful they have considerable healing powers, particularly helpful in recuperation.

Hiddenite

History and legend
The stone was named after W. E. Hidden, the American mineralogist who discovered it and identified it as a stone in its own right in 1879. According to popular tradition, hiddenite wards off lightning, and by extension sudden catastrophes.

Healing properties
This stone alleviates pain, strengthens the heart and blood circulation, relaxes tension in the shoulder and back area, and improves sight and hearing. It also eases rheumatic pain and strengthens the muscles. Psychologically, it is used to treat depression and anxiety. In addition, it gives a feeling of harmony and clarity of mind.

The pale green flat hiddenite crystals from Brazil are particularly powerful.

Magical properties
Hiddenite helps people who suffer from depression and anxiety.

This bright stone creates a feeling of harmony and helps its possessor see situations more clearly.

Chakra classification
Hiddenite should be used on the heart chakra. Lie on your back completely relaxed and place the hiddenite in the middle of your chest.

Star sign
Not associated with any particular star sign.

Application and care
Hiddenite should be cleansed once a week under warm running water and discharged in a bowl of sea salt. Then recharge it overnight among pointed rock crystals.

Hiddenite is a powerful healing stone. It should therefore be discharged and cleansed regularly.

Where found	USA, Brazil, Madagascar as well as Afghanistan
Color(s)	white to dark green, translucent
Chemical composition	LiAl [Si$_2$O$_6$]
Hardness	6
Available forms	the stone occurs only very rarely; hiddenite is used only as a rough stone or tumbled stone
Crystallization	a form of spodomene, it is a lithium-aluminum composite; monoclinic crystal

Hiddenite belongs to the pyroxene family. It takes its name from the geologist W. E. Hidden who discovered it in the United States in 1879 and defined it as a stone in its own right.

Iceland spar

History and legend

Viking seers used Iceland spar to help them in their predictions. They imported it from Iceland to the European mainland. Because of its characteristic of making objects appear double, Iceland spar was considered a mysterious stone. It symbolized peace, good fortune and friendship.

Healing properties

It is probably because of its high calcium content that this stone is frequently used to strengthen and promote healthy bones, teeth, hair, and nails. Other problems and disorders that can benefit from Iceland spar are skin inflammations, fungal infections and eczema. Iceland spar water (made by leaving the stone in a glass of water overnight) helps alleviate arthritis, rheumatism and back pain. Although the stone makes one see double, it also makes

Iceland spar is calcium carbonate, the material forming the bones of the human body.

the wearer more perceptive regarding false oaths and empty promises of love.

Magical properties
Named after its place of origin, Iceland spar symbolizes true love.

Chakra classification
Works well on the forehead and navel chakras.

Star sign
Not associated with any particular star sign.

Application and care
Once a month, it should be rinsed under warm running water and then recharged in the sun for several hours.

The high calcium content in the stone encourages healthy bones, skin, hair, nails and teeth.

Where found	Iceland, USA, Mexico
Color(s)	white, yellowish, pink; always refractive
Chemical composition	$CaCO_3$
Hardness	3
Available forms	only found as individual crystals
Crystallization	it is a variety of calcite; it is formed from pure calcium carbonate and can refract light twice; orthorhombic or hexagonal crystal

This variety of calcite has an interesting feature: its rhomboid crystals have a double light refraction effect which means that for instance printing seen through it appears doubled.

Iolite

History and legend

The ancient Greeks and Romans classified this stone as sapphire. Its name is derived from the Greek *ion*, meaning "violet," because of the color.

Healing properties

This stone can used to treat a wide variety of diseases and problems of the digestive tract. Feelings of bloat and heartburn, vomiting, stomach and bowel disorders can all be alleviated with it. Iolite can also strengthen the circulation and reduce blood pressure.

In addition it can prevent water retention and combat varicose veins. Psychologically, iolite reduces anxiety and depression in the wearer and also alleviates one of the curses of modern civilization, stress.

The refraction of light is a typical characteristic of iolite.

Magical properties

A distinctive characteristic of iolite is its play of color. As a result of its refractive properties, its color changes depending on the angle of observation, going from gray to sapphire blue and violet blue. This also reflects its many-layered healing properties.

Chakra classification

Put the iolite on the throat or forehead chakra for direct chakra healing.

Star sign

Not associated with any particular star sign.

Application and care

Iolite should be cleansed once a week under warm running water. Then it should be recharged among rock crystals or in the sun for a maximum of one hour.

Depending on the angle from which it is looked at, iolite appears transparent or opaque.

Where found	China, India, Madagascar, Sri Lanka, Brazil
Color(s)	gray, blue, violet
Chemical composition	$Mg_2Al_3 [AlSi_5O_{18}]$
Hardness	7
Available forms	it is used as rough stone and tumble stone; iolite is also a jewelry gemstone
Crystallization	composition of aluminum-magnesium ; its striking characteristic is its special refraction, so that the stone changes color according to the direction from which it is looked at; orthorhombic crystal

Iolite is also known as water sapphire because of its beautiful blue color. However it has nothing in common with true sapphire.

Jade (jadeite)

History and legend

Jade has been used and much sought after in China since 5000 B.C. The Chinese saw that it was harder and more resistant than any other stone known at the time. It was also easy to recognize because of its beautiful color, its surface, and the sound made when two stones were knocked against each other. The ancient Egyptians and Mayas believed it could arouse and preserve love.

Healing properties

Jade is believed to endow its possessor with the ability to interpret dreams.

Jade has blood-staunching properties, so women should wear a jade necklace during childbirth. It has a beneficial effect on all glandular functions, lowers fever and has a detoxifying effect on the body by stimulating the kidneys. Jade water should be drunk first thing in the morning. Psychologically, it calms, counteracts prejudices, and gives its possessor a sense of justice and contentment.

Magical properties
Jade symbolizes renewal. In Asia jade is still considered a lucky stone and frequently worn as an amulet.

Chakra classification
Should be used on the sacral or forehead chakra or on the solar plexus.

Star sign
Strongly recommended for Libra and also for Pisces and Cancer.

Application and care
Place jade on the forehead for quarter of an hour before going to sleep. If the stone becomes opaque or takes a while to warm up on the body, cleanse under running water. Recharge dry jade overnight in an amethyst geode.

Jade is said to promote fertility.

Where found	Burma, China, Canada, New Zealand; also found in small quantities in Mexico, Egypt and Silesia
Color(s)	light green to dark green, transparent; rarely: violet, yellow and black jade
Chemical composition	$NaAl\,[Si_2O_6] + Ca, Fe, Mg, Mn$
Hardness	6.5 to 7
Available forms	carved as artistic pieces; cut or shaped as pieces of jewelry; rough stone for putting water; amulets, usually as a pi (jade disk with a hole in the middle)
Crystallization	inclusions of chromium give this composition of sodium-aluminum its celebrated jade green color; it is formed from the metamorphosis of basic rocks; monoclinic crystal

In Chinese tradition jade symbolizes the five virtues of humanity: wisdom, justice, compassion, modesty and courage. Symbols of these virtues were carved from jade.

173

Jasper

History and legend

The ancient Egyptians wore jasper scarabs as amulets because the stone was believed to increase sexual energy. Massages with a round, polished jasper are said to have an aphrodisiac effect. According to the Bible, jasper was a direct gift from God and would be the first foundation stone of the New Jerusalem. Both Indians in Asia and Native Americans see jasper as a magical rain stone as well as a powerful healing stone for kidneys, liver and gall bladder.

Healing properties

When laid on therapeutically, red jasper stimulates sexuality and fertility, while when worn as a decorative necklace it combats exhaustion. Red-brown jasper is particularly beneficial in the treatment of liver, spleen, and pancreas. Drinking jasper water one hour before each meal is said to promote weight loss (place the stone

Red-brown jasper helps in cases of poor digestion.

every night in a glass of water and cover). To combat constipation, drink the whole glass of jasper water every second day first thing in the morning. Yellow jasper is particularly good for menopausal women who should drink the water every morning. In addition, yellow jasper strengthens the immune system.

Magical properties
Jasper symbolizes will power. In the Middle Ages it was the warrior's stone, and legend has it that it adorned Siegfried's sword.

Chakra classification
Yellow jasper works on the solar plexus, red jasper on the root chakra.

Star sign
Jasper is linked to Aries and Virgo.

Application and care
Jasper needs direct contact with the skin. After each use, the stone must be cleansed under running lukewarm water and recharged overnight in a bowl of tumbled hematite stones.

Mookaite combines the properties of red and yellow jasper.

Where found	yellow: India, Mexico; red: Black Forest; France, Egypt, USA, Africa, Australia, Brazil
Color(s)	yellow, red, reddish-brown, green; opaque
Chemical composition	SiO_2 + Fe, O, OH, Si
Hardness	7
Available forms	polished as a hand stone or for laying on the body; cut shapes worn as jewelry
Crystallization	fine-grained quartz, crytallized in trigonal aggregate, containing traces of many foreign substances; manganese gives it a yellow appearance and iron a strong red one; trigonal crystal

Red mookaite with white or yellowish speckled inclusions is a variation of jasper. It promotes good health and well-being, encouraging harmony and inner calm.

Jet

History and legend

A jet pendant worn over the heart should protect the wearer from scorpion and snake bites. Jet is known as a protective stone among North American Indians. They also use its comforting properties to help them after the death of a relative.

Healing properties

In addition to its protective qualities, the main physical ailments that can be alleviated by jet are arthritis and inflammation of the joints. It is also helpful in the treatment of bronchitis, colds, and headache.

Jet is coal that has become petrified in the course of millions of years.

Jet will provide great support and help alleviate the pain and suffering caused by separation or the death of loved ones. It also protects its possessor from enemies and evil thoughts while at the same time giving him new courage.

Magical properties

Jet is a protective stone that protects against evil spirits, magic spells and witchcraft. It should also protect its owner from enemies. In addition, it reflects and balances the ups and downs of the psyche.

Chakra classification

Jet is most effective and powerful when placed on the forehead chakra. In direct chakra therapy, you should lie on your back in a relaxed manner, place the stone in the middle of your forehead and concentrate on your forehead chakra.

Star sign

All signs benefit from its healing properties. Jet also works as a protective stone for all star signs.

Application and care

The stone is cleansed and recharged by placing it in sea salt one night and among rock crystals the next. Neither water nor sun should be used in its cleansing and charging.

Jet has a powerful healing effect on the respiratory tract.

Never use jet without first thoroughly discharging it. This is because, like all black stones, it can store good and bad forces.

Where found	USA, Brazil, Dominican Republic, former Soviet Union
Color(s)	black, opaque
Chemical composition	C (brown coal)
Hardness	2 to 3
Available forms	jet is used as a tumbled stone or it is often worn as jewelry in the form of pendants
Crystallization	it is simply petrified coal; amorphous stone

Kunzite

History and legend

This stone was discovered at the beginning of the twentieth century in America. It is named after its discoverer, the gemmologist G. F. Kunz. Although it does not have a long history, its effectiveness has been tried and proven.

Healing properties

Kunzite is a very powerful healing stone that has a beneficial effect on a wide range of disorders. It helps people who suffer from inner turmoil to achieve a balance between reason and feelings. It alleviates sciatica and painful joints when applied overnight, taped directly to the site of the pain. The regular drinking of kunzite water ensures a balanced production of blood corpuscles and healthy circulation. Violet kunzite regulates the activity of the thyroid gland and promotes hormonal balance. Pink kunzite prevents narrowing

Kunzite has a pronounced calming effect on the heart.

of the arteries, relaxes tense muscles, and alleviate rheumatism and arthritis. Kunzite is also very helpful in the treatment of drug and alcohol addiction. It promotes tolerance towards others. The ability to deal with criticism is improved, and the stone strongly stimulates self-development in the wearer.

Kunzite helps combat feelings of inferiority, inhibition, and depression.

Magical properties

Kunzite symbolizes straightforwardness. By increasing the wearer's tolerance, it also helps him form friendships.

Chakra classification

Pink kunzite is recommended for the heart chakra, violet kunzite for the forehead chakra.

Star sign

Not associated with any particular star sign.

Application and care

Kunzite should be worn directly on the skin. To relieve pain it should be placed directly on the place where it hurts. It should be cleansed under warm running water every time before use and recharged overnight among dry hematite stones.

Kunzite is a member of the pyroxene family of minerals which are formed in magmatic or metamorphic rocks. The name "pyroxene" is derived from the Greek words pyro *and* xene, *meaning "fire" and "foreign," or "foreign to fire."*

Where found	Brazil, Madagascar, Afghanistan, Myanmar and USA
Color(s)	white, pink, red, violet, transparent
Chemical composition	LiAl $[Si_2O_6]$ + Ca, Mg, Mn, Na
Hardness	6 to 7
Available forms	used in its natural form or cut and worked as jewelry; as a therapy stone it is carried next to the skin
Crystallization	kunzite is an aluminum acetate-lithium composition; its color comes from manganese; monoclinic crystal

Kyanite

History and legend

The name is derived from *kynos*, the Greek word for "blue." Because of its particular characteristic of developing different hardness in different directions, it was also given the name *disstenos*, which means dual hardness.

Because of its dark blue color, the ancient Greeks identified kyanite as the protective stone of seafarers. It was offered to those about to embark on long journeys.

Healing properties

Kyanite is ideal for wearing round the neck because it has beneficial effects on the throat. It promotes the ability to speak easily and express oneself and to learn languages. It removes energy blockages and stimulates vital energy. It is used to treat hearing disorders, eye problems and problems of sense of smell.

People who have to talk a lot should wear kyanite round the neck.

180

Psychologically, kyanite produces positive energy, sharpens the concentration and encourages calmness. It relaxes, drives away sadness and makes life seem more worth living.

Magical properties
Kyanite symbolizes lightness and leads to new thoughts.

Chakra classification
Placed on the throat chakra, kyanite lightens the soul and combats lack of feeling.

Star sign
Kyanite is associated with Aries, Taurus and Libra.

Application and care
After wearing or using for healing it should be cleansed under warm running water. Recharge among rock crystals.

Kyanite is the healing stone for the larynx, voice and speech.

Kyanite is found in several colors ranging from white to bluish-white, pale blue and intense blue. The deeper the blue the stronger its healing properties. The presence of crystal inclusions in the parent rock makes particularly powerful healing stones.

Where found	Finland, Austria, Switzerland, Italy, West Africa, Brazil, USA
Color(s)	from white to blue, occasionally also pink, yellow or green stripes
Chemical composition	$Al_2O_3 \cdot SiO_2$ + Ca, Cr, Fe, K, Mg, Ti
Hardness	4 to 7
Available forms	rough stone, tumbled stone (rarely), pendant
Crystallization	triclinic crystal structure

Labradorite

History and legend
Labradorite was discovered at the end of the eighteenth century on the Canadian peninsula of Labrador after which it was named. The particularly beautiful Finnish variety known as spectrolite was discovered in the twentieth century and soon became a sought-after gemstone because of its intense play of colors. It also has very good healing properties.

Healing properties
Labradorite stimulates the imagination and improves the memory.

Labradorite is very effective in alleviating bone problems, disorders of the spinal column, and wear and tear of the joints. Rheumatism and arthritis can also benefit from the stone's healing powers. Psychologically, labradorite has a calming, harmonizing effect, so it is a very good stone for irascible people. Labradorite improves intuition and clarifies the possessor's own views and objectives.

Finnish labradorite has the most beautiful colors.

Magical properties
With its shimmering play of colors Labradorite symbolizes fantasy and creativity. The stone's sparkle is reminiscent of fireworks.

Chakra classification
Labradorite works well on the navel chakra and the secondary chakras of the hands.

Star sign
The stone is linked to Aquarius.

Application and care
When intended for healing purposes labradorite should be carried around as a touchstone and then cleansed under running water. If its surface becomes cloudy, it should be put in mineral water and placed in the sun for a few days.

Where found	Finland, USA, Canada, Madagascar, Australia, former Soviet Union and Mexico
Color(s)	gray-blue stone, surface iridescent with all colors
Chemical composition	Na $[AlSi_3O_8]$/Ca$[Al_2Si_2O_8]$ + Fe, K, Ba, Sr
Hardness	6 to 6.5
Available forms	in modern architecture, labradorite is used as a highly polished iridescent reflecting stone; it us worn as a ring, brooch or pendant; for healing it is best carried as a touchstone
Crystallization	it belongs to the feldspar family and crystallizes from basic magmatic rock as a layered structure so that incident light is broken up, giving it its iridescence; triclinic crystal

Labradorite stimulates the thymus gland and stabilizes the body's own immune system. It is used in the treatment of colds.

Lapis lazuli

History and legend

The legends, reports, and stories surrounding lapis lazuli date back to 5000 B.C. For the Assyrians lapis lazuli was the holy stone Uknu, which brought the blue of the sky and with it the light of the gods to the earth. The word is a compound word made up of the Arabic *azul*, meaning "blue sky" and the Latin *lapis*, meaning "stone."

It was the stone of the ancient rulers. Burial objects made of lapis lazuli were found in the ancient royal tombs of Ur by the Euphrates. The French Sun King Louis XIV, Napoleon, and the German Emperor Wilhelm I also appreciated its special properties.

Lapis lazuli is a stone with medicinal properties related to the head.

Medicinal properties

It promotes clear understanding and intuition; it also helps the balanced functioning of the thyroid gland while strengthening the

neck and vocal cords. In addition it has hypotensive properties (never use lapis lazuli to treat people with low blood pressure). It is effective against depression, promotes bonding and strengthens idealism.

Magical properties
Blue lapis lazuli symbolizes inspiration and wisdom. Rulers wore it for its protective properties and as an ornament.

Chakra classification
This stone works well on the forehead and throat chakras.

Star sign
Lapis lazuli gives Sagittarius the power of friendship and helps him make decisions.

Application and care
Once a month lapis lazuli should be put in a bowl with tumbled hematite stones and then recharged in a mass of rock crystals.

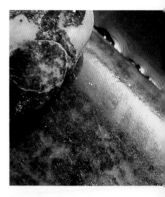

Lapis lazuli strengthens the immune system

Where found	Afghanistan, Myanmar, Chile, Lake Bakal
Color(s)	light blue, azure blue, violet-blue with speckled gold-colored inclusions, opaque
Chemical composition	$(Na, Ca)_8 [(S, SO_4, Cl_2)_2/(AlSiO_4)_6] + Fe$
Hardness	5 to 6
Available forms	rough stones for placing on the body, as an amulet for laying on the body, as carved figures and worked as jewelry
Crystallization	Lapis lazuli is formed by the conversion of lime to marble; several minerals are involved in the process; it is a sodium-silicate-aluminum composition that rarely forms individual crystals; the "gold" inclusions are pyrites; cubic crystal

All cultures have used this stone to decorate the statues of their divinities. It was also greatly valued by rulers, being used for magical and medicinal purposes.

Larimar

History and legend

The American Indians believed that Larimar brought luck and also had healing properties. The inhabitants of the Caribbean also believed it to be a lucky stone with healing properties. According to legend it is associated with lost paradise. It was subsequently thought to be the only remaining vestige of the legendary island Atlantis.

Larimar is a good stone for self-development.

Healing properties

Larimar is said to strengthen the bones. As a result it is often used to treat children and plays an important part in their children's growth. It also has beneficial effects on arthritis, hardening of the arteries and muscles, sciatica and lumbago. The stone breaks old thought patterns, frees and opens up new ways of thinking and acting. In addition, it protects against negative energy.

Magical properties
Larimar is also known as the Atlantis stone. It symbolizes bound-lessness and immensity. Its colors range from light blue to green-ish shades. Its palette of colors embodies the vastness of the sky and sea.

Chakra classification
Use Larimar on the throat chakra.

Star sign
The stone is linked to Leo.

Application and care
Larimar should be discharged once a week under warm running water. After cleansing it must recharged in the sun for at least one hour, either in the morning or evening.

If the stone changes color it is said to be particularly effective.

Larimar comes in various shades of blue ranging from pale blue to whitish-blue, and very rarely with a little green. The reserves of this stone have almost been depleted.

Where found	exclusively in the Dominican Republic
Color(s)	light blue to greenish
Chemical composition	$NaCa_2\,[OH/Si_3O_8]$ + Fe, Mn
Hardness	6
Available forms	larimar is mainly used as a tumbled stone; jewelry stones are also found commercially
Crystallization	it is a calcium-copper-magnesium silicate with triclinic crystal structure

Leopard jasper

History and legend

The reddish-beige leopard jasper is reminiscent of a leopard skin. It is particularly important in the culture of the Indians of the Americas. According to Indian belief Mexico was the center of the world. Because leopard jasper was found there, they also believed that their world was made of this stone. They believed that leopard jasper protected against wild animals. At the same time, they also believed that the stone harmonized the relationship between man and the animal world.

Leopard jasper reduces the passion for hunting and prevents the wearer from tormenting animals.

Healing properties

Leopard jasper stimulates the detoxification of the liver, gallbladder and bladder. It relaxes tension and alleviates abdominal pain. It helps stop hiccups and nausea. It also has many positive effects on the psyche. The stone brings about renewed harmony between

the wearer and his environment. It improves his power of endurance. In addition, it calms the wearer and at the same stimulates his imagination.

Chakra classification
Use the stone on the navel and sacral chakras.

Star sign
Not associated with any particular star sign.

Application and care
Cleanse the stone after use under running lukewarm water. Necklaces should be discharged in bowl of dry tumbled hematites. It can be recharged in the sun or among rock crystals, even over a long period.

Leopard jasper can lessen jealousy and anxiety in relationships.

Leopard jasper is distinguished by its characteristic pattern. It is a quartz and its pattern is caused by the presence of metals and minerals that have crystallized in the stone.

Where found	Australia, Mexico, South Africa
Color(s)	reddish-beige (reminiscent of a leopard's skin)
Chemical composition	SiO_2
Hardness	7
Available forms	tumbled stone, touchstone; leopard jasper is also worked as a gemstone for jewelry, particularly as a pendant, necklace, sphere
Crystallization	trigonal crystal

Magnesite

History and legend

Magnesite was first discovered in Africa. In African cultures it is perceived as a fertility stone, while in ancient Egypt it was believed to be a lucky talisman.

Healing properties

A very good stone for overweight people because it stimulates the metabolism of fat and lowers cholesterol. In addition, it has very relaxing properties so that it is highly effective in the treatment of headaches, migraines and stomach and intestinal cramps.

Magical properties

Magnesite consists almost entirely of pure magnesium.

The white color symbolizes purity and freedom but also fertility. It is said to protect the wearer against false love, false friends and intrigues.

Chakra classification

The power of magnesite works well on the secondary chakras of the knees and hands.

Star sign

Magnesite is linked to Libra.

Application and care

Magnesite must be worn directly on the skin. It must be cleansed regularly under running warm water and recharged overnight by placing it among rock crystals.

Because of its high magnesium content, magnesite plays an important part in the formation of new bone.

Where found	Austria, Greece, Poland, Russia, USA, China
Color(s)	white to yellowish
Chemical composition	$MgCO_3$ + Ca, Fe, Mn
Hardness	4 to 4.5
Available forms	rough stone and tumbled stone; also worked as a stone for jewlery
Crystallization	magnesite originates primarily from the weathering of rocks containing magnesium, for instance serpentine, in which it forms dense fine-grained pieces of debris; it is also formed by the metasomatic replacement of dolomite or as crystalline inclusions occurring in the regional metmorphosis of lime; trigonal crystal

Magnesite promotes relaxation and a positive attitude to life. It removes negative feelings, reduces over-sensitivity and lifts depression.

Magnetite

History and legend

In ancient Greece this stone was called *magnetis*. With time people realized that the stone concealed both a positive and a negative magnetic pole, so it was a natural magnet. The healing properties of magnetite were already known in the early Middle Ages to Hildegard von Bingen (1098–1179). It is still used today in naturopathy and medicine.

Healing properties

Magnetite is used very successfully in treating quite different disorders. It is used in the treatment of lung infections, rheumatism, and liver disorders. But it will also improve a low blood count and accelerate the mending of bone fractures. Direct application to the affected site has a positive effect on the healing process. In addition, it has a positive influence on the psyche:

Magnetite is mined as crude ore all over the world.

the stone teaches its possessor to overcome conflicts and achieve inner harmony.

Magical properties
Black, opaque magnetite symbolizes freedom. Its magnetic property was known to the ancient Greeks.

Chakra classification
When placed on the crown chakra, magnetite promotes relaxation and harmony.

Star sign
Not associated with any particular star sign.

Application and care
Because the stone contains iron it must not come into contact with water. It should be discharged at nighttime among tumbled hematite stones and recharged with a magnet. It should be cleansed once a month with dry sea salt.

The opaque, metallic, shiny black color is a characteristic feature of magnetite.

Where found	Sweden, Norway, Switzerland, Elba, Brazil
Color(s)	black, metallic and opaque
Chemical composition	Fe_3O_4
Hardness	6
Available forms	rough stones are more common than gemstones for jewelry
Crystallization	cubic crystal

The stone consists of a highly concentrated iron oxide and in its purest form it develops octahedral crystals that are a good way of recognizing it.

Malachite

History and legend

The ancient Egyptians obtained their malachite from the Sinai peninsula and used it in amulets. In the *Egyptian Book of the Dead* it is
said that the goddess of the sky "drops stars on the earth in the shape
of green stones." In Alpine regions malachite has for centuries been
used to help expectant mothers and women in labor. The first cross-
es decorated with malachite date from the sixteenth century and
have now become popular collector's items.

Healing properties

The strongly striped, dark green stone promotes harmonious relationships.

Malachite promotes growth and builds up strength. This is why it
is the stone of pregnant women. In addition, it is a successful
remedy against heart pains and cardiac asthma. The optic nerves
can be strengthened by bathing the eyes daily with malachite
water. Malachite is also helpful psychologically, especially in cases

of lovesickness. It promotes understanding and spirituality, stimulating concentration.

Magical properties
Malachite symbolizes understanding of oneself and of others. That is why it is an ideal meditation stone.

Chakra classification
Malachite is effective on all chakras, particularly the heart chakra.

Star sign
Malachite is a lucky stone for Virgo and Capricorn.

Application and care
Malachite essence is very powerful and should be drunk daily, starting with one mouthful and gradually increasing to one glass. Malachite is strong enough to work when carried. To discharge, wrap the stone in a handkerchief and leave overnight among dry tumbled stones. To recharge, put the stone among rock crystals.

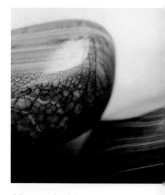

Most malachite objects, gemstones, and tumbled stones come from Zaire.

Because malachite is not a very hard stone, it can be ground into powder form. Its intense green color was used in the past as eye make-up and in fresco paintings.

Where found	in the vicinity of copper mines in Zaire, Israel (where it is known as the Eilat stone), USA, Australia, former Soviet Union, South-West Africa
Color(s)	light green to strong green, usually banded
Chemical composition	$Cu_2CO_3(OH)_2 + H_2O + (Ca, Fe)$
Hardness	3.5 to 4
Available forms	rough stone and polished, for laying on the body, as a touchstone, as jewelry
Crystallization	a basic copper carbonate, it forms a monoclinic structure in needle crystals or fibrous aggregates

Marcasite and Apache gold

History and legend
The Greeks called Apache gold pyrite agate. They knew that pyrite agate and marcasite were not really gold and therefore referred to them as yellow mica.

The Apaches used Apache gold as a good luck stone and for ritual purposes that protected them against illness and death in battle. Pyrite agate and marcasite produce glowing, fiery sparks when they are rubbed against each other.

Healing properties
These stones stimulate the release and elimination of toxic substances. They are used to treat poor digestion and loss of appetite. The stones are known to relieve catarrh, throat infection, and tonsillitis. When placed on the neck, they open up the respiratory tract and cure bronchitis. Marcasite placed in water that is then

The name pyrite agate is derived from the Greek word pyr, *which means "fire."*

used to gargle will help cure gum infections and inflammation of the mucus membranes of the mouth. Both stones bring peace and harmony to the wearer. Marcasite helps one to make decisions quickly and recognize priorities. Apache gold leads to clear thinking and removes psychological blockages.

Apache gold was a good luck stone for Native Americans, encouraging large families with many children.

Chakra classification

Apache gold and marcasite are very good for the solar plexus,

Star sign

Not associated with any particular star sign.

Application and care

These stones should not be cleansed in water but placed overnight in a bowl filled with hematite stones. This should be done once a month. They will be charged by the addition of a few clear rock crystals tips to the hematite stones. Do not charge in the sun.

Apache gold was confused with real gold by American Indians. It was later discovered that this mineral was pyrite agate.

Where found	Apache gold: Arizona, New Mexico; marcasite: Germany, Hungary, Sweden, Canada, USA, Mexico, Australia
Color(s)	gray-gold, golden with light and dark inclusion
Chemical composition	FeS_2
Hardness	6 to 6.5
Available forms	tumbled stones, ornamental stones, touchstone
Crystallization	Apache gold: iron-sulfur composition, rarely as crystals; marcasite: with addition of cobalt, zinc, silver, gold, in various crystals and crystal groups

Marcasite nodules

History and legend

Marcasite nodules owe their reputation as magic stones to their almost perfectly round shape. Because the stone was formed in the silt of dried-up lakes and not in the rock it is extremely rare. If only for that reason they are thought to bring their finder luck. These nodules are also known as "boji stones" and "living stones."

Healing properties

There are no precise guidelines for treating serious conditions. If the nodule contains visible pyrite crystals it is called a male stone; otherwise it is a female stone. Holding a male stone in one hand and a female one in the other is said to create a field of energy in the body that alleviates pain and removes blockages. It is also used as a preventative treatment, producing energy and removing psychological blockages. It is not used to treat serious disorders.

Male and female marcasite nodules create a powerful field of energy for the aura and body.

Magical properties

Marcasite nodules symbolize the principle of yin and yang because there are female and male "living stones," depending on whether they contain visible cube-shaped pyrite crystals (male) or not (female).

Chakra classification

A marcasite nodule is a very powerful stone that conveys energy to all the chakras.

Star sign

Marcasite nodules are not associated with a particular star sign. All star signs can use it as a source of energy.

Application and care

These energy stones must never be charged and do not need to be cleansed in water. They need only to be rubbed with a brush. They should always be kept at distance from pure iron.

Marcasite nodules thrive in the company of other precious stones and crystals.

Where found	USA
Color(s)	metallic gray
Chemical composition	FeS_2 + FeOOH + H_2O
Hardness	7.4 (although its composite metals are all softer)
Available forms	there are male and female stones; cubic prites crystals are visible in the male stones but not in the female ones; insist on a certificate of authenticity when buying!
Crystallization	pyrite ball with a covering of limonite; as a result of weathering cubic pyrites crystals are visible in the male stone but not in the female one; cubic crystal

Marcasite nodules are particularly popular in the United States. They should be treated like living beings: they need love, attention and kindness. If they do not receive this, they will turn to dust.

Mica

History and legend
Mica particles come to symbolize false sparkle and glitter.

Healing properties
The healing properties of mica depend on its color and they vary enormously. Pink and violet stones (lepidolite) are used in the treatment of liver complaints. They can also be used to detoxify the organism. Black stones (muscovite) can help in the case of gastro-intestinal disorders, diabetes, and colds. Green stones (fuchsite) promote a healthy blood count and help in the treatment of anemia and leukemia while also combating bone disease.

Green mica can also have a beneficial effect on the psyche. Restless people become calmer and lethargic people become more active.

The sparkling black mica is also called muscovite.

Magical properties

The violet and pink varieties are called lepidolite and have powerful protective properties. The blue-gray variety is called muscovite and encourages belief in the future.

Chakra classification

The pink-violet variety works on the forehead chakra, the black-gray works on the throat chakra, and the green on the heart chakra.

Star sign

Helps all star signs.

Application and care

If the stone changes color, it means that it must be thoroughly cleansed. To do this, rub the stone vigorously under running warm water. Otherwise, it can be discharged in a bowl filled with tumbled hematite stones and recharged among rock crystals for one hour or less in the sun.

Its effect depends on its color.

Where found	Sweden, Norway, Brazil, USA, South Africa, Australia as well as the former Soviet Union
Color(s)	pink, violet, brilliant gray through black, green
Chemical composition	the micas belong to the layer silicate-family and exist in several varieties
Hardness	2 to 2.5
Available forms	Rough stone, tumbled stone, touchstone; also as tabular crystals
Crystallization	metallic potassium-aluminum compostion; monoclinic crystal

Mica comes in a wide range of colors. A delicate structure is typical of mica, which is made up of numerous extremely thin layers.

Moonstone

History and legend

In antiquity the moonstone was called *selenitis*. Pliny wrote that "it showed a picture of the moon and its daily waning and waxing." Being associated with the moon, it has always been the stone of love and lovers. In Arab countries, a moonstone is offered as a "blessing" to ensure a large family and encourage the fertility of the woman. Even today, a moonstone is sewn into women's nightdresses so that it can exert its power.

Magical properties

The most beautiful moonstones come from Sri Lanka and India.

Moonstone promotes a natural, strong hormonal balance in women. It alleviates menstrual pain, promotes fertility and ensures an easy pregnancy and delivery. It is also very helpful for menopausal women. It has a beneficial effect on the lymphatic system, strengthens the immune system, and alleviates

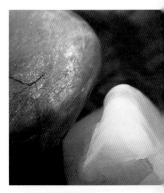

thyroid problems. In addition, it stimulates the production of hormones and has a positive effect on the glands and ensures good digestion. This stone promotes feminine characteristics and stimulates love and sensitivity. It diminishes anxiety, including concern about the future. It encourages zest for life and a youthful attitude even in old age. In addition, it brings inner harmony to its wearer.

Chakra classification
The moonstone is most effective on the sacral chakra.

Star sign
Moonstone has a positive influence on Cancer while bluish moonstone is effective for Pisces.

Moonstone is a very powerful healing stone for women.

Application and care
Moonstone is first and foremost a woman's stone. The stone should be carried on the person and discharged among dry tumbled hematite stones after each menstruation. It should be recharged on the window sill when the moon is full.

Where found	Sri Lanka, Brazil, Madagascar and USA
Color(s)	eggshell-colored, yellowish, bluish, blue
Chemical composition	$K\,[AlSi_3O_8]$ + Ba, Fe, Na
Hardness	6 to 6.5
Available forms	it is always cut, to bring out its sheen; very popular as a jewelry stone and amulet stone
Crystallization	the moonstone belongs to the feldspar family and crystallises as a monoclinic silicate structure, with an inner layered structure that breaks up the light, thus causing the stone's milky moonshine effect

There are many legends about moonstone. Its mysterious shimmering sparkle has captured human imagination for thousands of years.

Moqui marbles

History and legend
Moqui marbles are legendary stones from North America. They were believed to be stones from the heart of the earth. Moreover, they were stones that did not regenerate. They are identified as female stones, which are round and spherical with a smooth surface, and male stones, which are flat and disk-like with a rough surface.

Healing properties
Moqui marbles are a powerful source of energy, especially when they are held in pairs, for instance in your hands, during meditation. When picked up, the energy of the stones increases and can be transmitted to others. They can sharpen the eye and knowledge of what is right and natural, helping the owner develop greater inner calm and harmony.

The name Moqui has been translated as "faithful darling."

Magical properties

When used in pairs, the stones can give the owner an energy of an almost supernatural kind. If no attention is paid to them, the stones will turn to dust or disappear entirely.

Chakra classification

Moqui marbles are not linked to any particularly chakra. Simply hold them in your hands during meditation.

Star sign

Not associated with any particular star sign.

Application and care

Moqui marbles should not be stored in a cupboard or drawer. One must pay attention to them and handle them very frequently.

Charge the stone by exposing it to light and stroking it.

Where found	mainly USA (Utah)
Color(s)	granite-like appearance, shining according to its metal alloy composition
Chemical composition	SiO_2 + metal alloys of various compositions, mainly manganese, iron, titanium, palladium
Hardness	7.4 – although the components of the alloy are much softer; but only with a hardness of over 7 are the stones able to emerge "alive" and fully formed from within the earth
Available forms	Moqui marbles are sold with a certificate of authenticity; they are still being found
Crystallization	trigonal crystal

The Indians are particularly secretive about the sites where these stones are found, guarding them like precious treasure. Indian families keep a pair of stones to protect them against evil and false friends.

Moss agate

Healing properties

The healing power of moss agate has only been written about in recent years. It stimulates insulin production by the pancreas and thus combats diabetes and regulates the metabolism. The cleansing power of the kidneys and lymph system is improved by regularly drinking moss agate water. This also has a beneficial effect on the digestion. The immune system is thereby strengthened and the body is less prone to bacterial and viral infections.

Women also benefit from moss agate during pregnancy, labor, and while breast-feeding, because it is thought to enlarge the womb, open the vagina and activate the mammary glands.

Moss agate stimulates the production of insulin.

Moss agate strengthens the bonds with nature and promotes communication and understanding. This stone helps those who want to free themselves from long-established ways of life or dependencies such as addiction.

Magical properties

Moss agate is a lucky stone for gamblers. It is also said that a change in the play of colors warns its possessor against false friends.

Chakra classification

The heart chakra reacts well to moss agate.

Star sign

Moss agate has a particularly favorable influence on Capricorn.

Application and care

It will only develop its energy when in direct contact with the skin. It must be discharged under warm running water and, if possible, recharged overnight once a month among rock crystals.

Moss agate, in the form of a necklace or pendant, can free its wearer from addiction.

Where found	USA, India, China and in smaller quantities in South Africa and Brazil
Color(s)	milky white to red clear agate with mossy green inclusions
Chemical composition	SiO_2 + Al, Ca, F, Fe, K, Mg, Na, OH, Si
Hardness	6.5 to 7
Available forms	polished as a touchstone and talisman; it is available cut as a jewelry gemstone
Crystallization	as an agate, it belongs to the chalcedony quartz family, with a microcrystalline trigonal structure; usually it is formed in cleavage fractures of granite; the addition of hornblende and manganese create the characteristic green moss effect

Moss agate belongs to the agate family. The stones have a milky appearance, sometimes red in parts, with the characteristic green moss-like inclusions caused by the presence of manganese and hornblende.

Nephrite

History and legend
The name is derived from the Greek *nephron* (kidneys) because of the stone's particular power to cure kidney diseases. In South America nephrite was a very ancient ritual cult stone that is still highly valued as a protective stone. The Mayas believed that it staved off wounds. In ancient China, cut into a heart shape and worn on the chest, it protected against external and internal wounds. In ancient civilizations nephrite was often used to make weapons that were further decorated with magic signs.

Healing properties
Chronic bladder infections, irritable bladder syndrome and incontinence respond well to being treated with nephrite. The stone has a wide range of beneficial psychological effects: it makes the wearer more creative, calmer and more relaxed. It protects against

Nephrite water, drunk in the morning, is said to improve vision.

aggression and helps the wearer maintain his own identity even in difficult situations. At night, a flat nephrite placed under the pillow protects against nightmares. The stone also brings hope, personal happiness, professional success and recognition.

Magical properties
Nephrite protects against false friends and makes the wearer immune to love spells.

Chakra classification
Nephrite works well on the heart and throat chakras.

Star sign
Nephrite has a positive influence on Cancer.

Application and care
In acute cases nephrite should be taped in place overnight or worn as an amulet directly on the skin over a long period. The stone should only be discharged (under warm running water) and recharged (by being placed for a few hours in weak sunlight) when it becomes cloudy.

Used over a long period of time, nephrite will give its possessor inner peace.

Where found	New Zealand, Canada, Australia, China, USA
Color(s)	green and greenish-gray, opaque, sometimes speckled
Chemical composition	$Ca_2 (Mg, Fe)_5 [(OH, F)/Si_4O_{11}]_2$
Hardness	6 to 6.5
Available forms	tumbled stone, touchstone, also as a pendant
Crystallization	deposited as layers of compressed crystal structures of calcium-magnesium silicates, that are found in layers of slate; monoclinic crystal

Nephrite can strengthen the kidneys and cure kidney diseases. In this case a nephrite disk is taped in position over the kidney region.

Obsidian

History and legend
In the Stone Age obsidian was used to make weapons and blades.

Healing properties
This stone helps alleviate pain, reduce tension and release energy. It can also help staunch blood and accelerate the healing of wounds. Because it improves circulation, it is very good for cold feet and hands. It can be used to treat trauma, shock and anxiety attacks.

Magical properties
Obsidian has been used in magic rituals since time immemorial. In fortune telling obsidian is used as a mirror.

Chakra classification
Classification depends on the color and luster. Obsidian with

The coloring of obsidian is caused by the presence of titanium, iron or manganese.

black or gold shimmering is particularly effective on the forehead chakra, obsidian with dark brown shimmering works on the foot and hand chakras. Obsidian with rainbow shimmering works on all chakras.

Star sign
Obsidian is associated with Scorpio and Sagittarius.

Application and care
Obsidian is discharged once a month under warm running water and then recharged in the sun or among rock crystals.

Related stones
The mahogany-brown stone with black inclusions is called mahogany obsidian. It promotes logical thought, protects against anxiety and creates inner equilibrium. It also has anti-bacterial properties. It protects against inflammation and reduces allergies and infections while improving blood circulation.

Mahogany obsidian promotes the ability to think logically.

Where found	all regions where there have been volcanic eruptions
Color(s)	the various colors of lava flow
Chemical composition	$SiO_2 + Fe_2O_3 + H_2O$ + Al, C, Ca, Fe, K, Na
Hardness	5.5
Available forms	rough stone and tumbled stone, pendant, spheres, chakra disks and pyramids
Crystallization	amorphous, that is, it does not have a crystalline structure because it is formed by the rapid solidification of lava, rich in silicic acid, as it comes into contact with cold water.

Mahogany obsidian should be used on the hand and ankle chakras. It is particularly recommended for all Scorpios.

Olivine

History and legend

In antiquity olivine was imported from the volcanic island of Zebir-get in the Red Sea. It is said that Moses wore an olivine in his cuirass as protection. In the Middle Ages Hildegard von Bingen (1098–1179) declared that peridot, another name for olivine, was one of the "foundation" stones.

Healing properties

Olivine strengthens and protects the organs in the thorax, especially the heart and lungs. It also improves the immune system by stimulating the thymus gland. An olivine necklace, worn directly on the skin, protects against dehydration and brittleness. Psychologically, olivine creates inner harmony and combats envy and resentment. It helps to reduce anger, encourages admission of one's own faults, and helps the wearer make amends. Negative

The translucent olivine, usually olive green in color, is a very powerful stone.

feelings such as selfishness and coldness are transformed into positive feelings. It successfully combats sadness, melancholy and depression.

Magical properties
Olivine symbolizes cheerfulness and promotes friendship.

Chakra classification
Olivine is most effective on the heart chakra.

Star sign
Olivine has a positive influence on those born under the sign of Cancer.

Application and care
Olivine should be discharged every day under running water and recharged in the sun for a few hours if possible.

Unknotted olivine necklaces increase the healing power of olivine.

Where found	in eroded lava: clear crystals of warm green color from Egypt; in addition: Norway, Arizona, Myanmar, the Eifel mountains in Germany, Vesuvius in Italy, and Lanzarote
Color(s)	olive green to yellow
Chemical composition	$(Mg, Fe)_2 [SiO_4]$ + Al, Ca, Mn, Ni, Co, Cr, Ti
Hardness	6.5 to 7
Available forms	cut as a valued jewelry gemstone; small pieces found in lava sand are kept in linen bags as healing stones
Crystalliation	olivine is an orthorhombic prismatic crystal of magnesium-iron-silicate composition, sometimes with rounded corners; translucent to transparent

Olivine, also known as chrysolite and peridot, is usually only found in small, friable pieces. Translucent stones and crystals as large as a finger nail are becoming increasingly rare.

Onyx

History and legend

Polished onyx develops a pattern with shapes that look a little like eyes because of the white inclusions. As a result, it has been used for thousands of years for healing eye disorders, as described in the books by Konrad von Megenberg (1309–74), rector of the Vienna Stefansschule and canon of Regensburg. In antiquity onyx was considered one of the most important healing stones.

Healing properties

Onyx must be laid on the body or worn or over a long period because its power develops very slowly. Onyx is particularly effective on the skin, healing infected wounds as well as fungal infections, inflammation, and even sunburn. Pat the affected skin with onyx water several times during the day and cover with an onyx water compress at night. Onyx also works on the psyche,

Black onyx penetrates strongly through the skin.

deflecting negative energy, increasing the wearer's stamina, and giving him inner harmony. It promotes self-confidence and a sense of responsibility and helps its possessor achieve success.

Magical properties

It is used as a magic stone all over the world. Its power is further increased by magic inscriptions, as found in the graves of American Indians and ancient Greeks and Romans.

Chakra classification

Onyx influences all the chakras. If possible combine it with other stones whose power it increases.

Star sign

Onyx has a positive influence on Capricorn.

Application and care

Onyx needs time to develop its full power. It should be discharged once a week under running water and, if used for a long period, it should be placed in the earth overnight once a month.

Since antiquity onyx has been used as a protection against black magic.

Where found	Brazil, India, Madagascar, USA, Mexico
Color(s)	black, opaque
Chemical composition	SiO_2 + C, Fe
Hardness	7
Available forms	polished as a touchstone or as a healing stone for laying on the body; cut and worked as a jewelry stone
Crystallization	as an agate, onyx belongs to the quartz family; it is an oxide and forms trigonal crystals in fibrous aggregates

Black, barely translucent onyx has no connection with the yellow, brown, and green stones that are often mistakenly called onyx but are in fact varieties of calcite-aragonite.

Opal

History and legend
Pliny the Elder described the opal thus: "It combines the soft fire of the carbuncle, the shimmering purple of the amethyst, the beautiful sea-green of the emerald, the golden yellow of the topaz, and the deep blue of the sapphire so that all the colors sparkle together in a wonderful play of colors." In mythology the gods saw it as the embodiment of the beauty of all precious stones. Opals were said to contain the tears shed by Zeus after his victory over the Titans.

Healing properties

Opal's colors are created by microscopic water drops within the stone.

Linked to the heart, stomach and digestion, it stimulates the glands and regulates the acids and enzymes in the metabolism. Opal also has a beneficial effect on the psyche, pouring balm on broken hearts and restoring inner harmony. In meditation opal is one of the most powerful stones for the soul.

Magical properties
In India opal is considered a lucky stone; in the Far East it is a symbol of eternal hope, but at times its iridescence is also seen as a presage of bad luck and witchcraft.

Chakra classification
The crown chakra is receptive to the energy of the opal.

Star sign
The opal is linked to Pisces and Cancer.

Application and care
The opal must not be used in combination with other stones. It will lose its sparkling shimmer if it comes into contact with perfume, soap or make-up. Soak frequently in water for half an hour; do not recharge in the sun but among rock crystals.

Moss opal is most effective on the heart chakra.

Where found	South Australia, Mexico, Brazil
Color(s)	colorless, white, blue, green, red, crimson, yellow, black; usually but not invariably opalescent, so that it gleams with all the colors of the rainbow
Chemical composition	$SiO_2 + H_2O + Ca, C, Fe, Mg$
Hardness	5.5 to 6.5
Available forms	jewelry stone for carrying, laying on the body as a healing stone, as the object of meditation
Crystallization	the opal is usually formed in fissures in volcanic rock; it is a silicon dioxide of amorphous form that only rarely forms grape-like crystals; its opalescent quality is formed by microscopically small water drops under the surface of the stone; amorphous rock

The pale blue, often beige-colored moss opal with its dark sediments, stimulates the production of insulin, regulates the metabolism and strengthens the body's own defenses, reducing inflammation and lowering fever.

Orpiment

History and legend

The name is derived from the Latin *orpimentum*, which means "gold colored." In Asia orpiment was used as a color pigment and for religious marking on the forehead. It was also taken internally during ceremonies as a love potion or elixir of immortality. Only experienced medicine men were allowed to prepare this because of orpiment's poisonous nature.

Healing properties

It is vitally important to make sure that the stone is not ingested. Orpiment contains the poison arsenic and must never be taken internally!

Orpiment is used on the forehead chakra during meditation.

It is applied externally as a powder to treat sexual disorders, which often go hand in hand with a lack of *joie de vivre*. It is said to cure frigidity, ovarian disorders, and hormonal unbalance. It also

encourages social activities and brings new energy to long-standing relationships.

Magical properties
Orpiment has a magical color. In the past it was used in love potions and elixirs intended to confer immortality.

Chakra classification
Orpiment is ideal for using on the third eye.

Star sign
Suitable for all star signs.

Application and care
It should never be placed in the sun and must be charged among rock crystals.

Orpiment exists in various shades of ranging from lemon to red-yellow.

Where found	China, Japan, USA
Color(s)	lemon yellow, reddish yellow
Chemical composition	As_2S_3
Hardness	1 to 2
Available forms	orpiment is used as a powder or as a rough stone for laying on the body
Crystallization	orpiment occurs in fibrous crystals and distintegrates into powder under the influence of light; monoclinic crystal

All orpiment in the various shades of yellow contain poisonous arsenic and is therefore very dangerous. Used externally, it is completely safe.

Orthoclase

History and legend

Orthoclase only arrived late in Europe. It was first discovered in Africa where it was washed ashore along the eastern coast. Today it is found mainly in Madagascar. People in Africa valued orthoclase as a powerful healing and protective stone. They were convinced that its pale, lemon yellow sparkle gave protection against spirits bringing bad luck.

Healing properties

The precious yellow orthoclase is found mainly in Madagascar.

The yellow to lemon yellow transparent orthoclase is the ideal healing stone for problems affecting older people. It drives away the fear of aging and promotes mental agility and optimism well into old age. It protects the inner organs of the body and prevents premature organ deterioration. It also strengthens the bones and protects against rheumatic pain, painful joints and arthritis. The

stone helps age-related problems with vision, cardiac weakness, circulatory problems, even senility. Orthoclase will also help prevent dehydration of the skin. On a psychological level, orthoclase drives away anxiety about the future, especially that related to aging. It brings a new sense of happiness and contentment, giving the possessor a new perspective on life. Its powerful vibrations promote optimism and a more active mental life.

A necklace of orthoclase helps reduce the fear of aging.

Chakra classification
Orthoclase is most effective on the navel chakra.

Star sign
Not associated with any particular star sign.

Application and care
It should be discharged and cleansed once a week under lukewarm running water. Afterwards recharge the stone for a few hours among rock crystals.

Orthoclase alerts its possessor to changes in the body so that organ deficiencies do not occur without warning.

Where found	Madagascar, Germany, Italy
Color(s)	lemon yellow, transparent
Chemical composition	$K\,[AlSi_3O_8]$
Hardness	6
Available forms	crystal, tumbled stone, touchstone; orthoclase is also used in jewelry, usually in pendants
Crystallization	monoclinic crystal

Pearl

History and legend

A pearl necklace worn four thousand years ago by the Persian queen Achemenid can still be admired today. The pearl jewelry of the Queen of Sheba has become legendary. It is said that Cleopatra served wine with ground pearls in it to her more important guests. The Bible says, "The price of wisdom is above pearls" (Job 28. 18). And Lucifer is said to have broken his teeth because of his craving for pearls. Pearls actually belong to the marine animal kingdom, but most people consider them precious stones.

Healing properties

The pearl has always been the symbol of woman's perfect beauty.

Drinking pearl water regularly over a long period stabilizes the production of hormones. Chronic headaches and migraines can be alleviated or completely cured by wearing a pearl necklace directly on the skin. Pearls also reduce allergies. Psychological-

ly, pearls promote wisdom and contentment well into old age.

Magical properties
A pearl necklace is believed to warn sensitive people of imminent disaster.

Chakra classification
Pearls are related to Cancer. Black pearls are linked to Capricorn.

Application and care
Pearls should be worn on the skin and not be allowed to come into contact with perfume or make-up. Without regular contact with the skin they become dull. And when not worn, the pearls should not be stored in the dark (for instance, in a drawer). Pearls must be discharged overnight in salt sea water and recharged in an oyster shell.

Produced by oysters, the pearl belongs to the marine animal kingdom.

Where found	Persian Gulf, coasts of Central America and north Australia, Gulf of Mannar
Color(s)	silver, cream, and gold, becoming green, blue, black, always gleaming
Chemical composition	$CaCO_3$ + organic substances
Hardness	3 to 4
Available forms	loose pearls, pearl necklaces
Crystallization	consists of calcium carbonate and the organic substances of oysters, mother-of-pearl, that provides iridescence; it accumulates when a foreign body such as a grain of sand penetrates an oyster

Precious pearl jewelry, much loved by kings, emperors, tsars, maharajahs, and princes, can be admired in museums throughout the world.

Petrified wood

History and legend
Petrified wood is formed from the petrifaction of primeval trees, the giant sequoias, that have remained airtight for millions of years. In ancient times the Etruscans treated them as cult objects. Today, they are used by followers of esoteric traditions to recall memories of former lives.

Healing powers
Petrified wood stabilizes the health and the body's defenses. It generates calm and encourages contentment. The wood helps preserve a sense of healthy roots.

The petrified wood of the giant sequoia is found in many strong earth colors.

Magical properties
In mythology, petrified wood is regarded as an object with divine power and a symbol of man's connection to the natural world.

Chakra classification
Petrified wood provides energy to the heart chakra.

Star signs
Not associated with any particular star sign.

Application and use
Petrified wood is cleansed with water and charged for a short time (thrity minutes) in the sun.

Tree quartz exists as rough stones, touchstones and pendants.

Related stones
Tree quartz is a petrified branch with bark, whose formation began over 150 million years ago through the amalgamation of silicic acid with a dead tree. In the course of time the mineral-rich liquid solidifies and the wood becomes petrified. The reddish-brown orange tree quartz with its grayish-white bark is found only in Madagascar. Tree quartz has only a few known healing properties but it can deliver very intense energy to the root chakra. It is discharged under warm running water and recharged among rock crystals.

The amorphous tree quartz works on the root chakra and protects from arteriosclerosis and constricted veins. Tree quartz water taken on a calm stomach stimulates the circulation and nervous system.

Where found	USA (Arizona), Brazil, Australia, Canada, Africa, Germany
Color(s)	gray-brown, brown, from sequoia trees, as well as in strong colors (brown, red, violet, blue, green, yellow)
Chemical composition	SiO_2 (C, Fe, OH)
Hardness	depending on the wood
Available forms	petrified wood exists in rough form or as spheres, pyramids and pendants
Crystallization	dead wood solidifies in the earth without oxygen under the influence of silicic acid and turns into quartz or opal; amorphous stone

Phantom quartz

History and legend
Phantom quartz takes its name from the particular structure of its crystallization: each crystal displays the outlines of numerous smaller crystals, known as phantoms. It is a rock crystal that in the course of millions of years has formed over earlier rock crystals that already existed.

Healing properties
Phantom quartz is a very powerful healing stone. Because of its multiple crystallization it is even more powerful than rock crystal. Apart from that phantom quartz has the same properties as rock crystal. In addition, it helps in cases of nervous insomnia. Psychologically, it protects against bad influences and anxiety. It increases the possessor's perception and ability to take things in. The way phantom quartz has developed makes it particularly

Many phantom quartz crystals reveal the presence of several generations of rock crystals inside them.

suitable for helping its possessor to overcome limitations and remove mental blocks.

Chakra classification
Phantom quartz invigorates the aura: simply place it next to you during meditation.

Star sign
Not associated with any particular star sign.

Application and care
Phantom quartz crystals, spheres or large individual crystals set in silver, are particularly powerful. Cleanse and dischage at least once a week under warm running water if worn on the body. After being discharged they can be recharged for a few hours in the midday sun.

Phantom quartz is a good meditation stone, strengthening the aura.

Where found	Switzerland, Austria, USA, Brazil, Madagascar
Color(s)	like rock crystal, but several crystals grown together
Chemical composition	SiO_2
Hardness	7
Available forms	crystal groups, individual crystals, crystal points, touchstone, tumbled stones; as a jewelry gemstone, usually found in the form of a pendant
Crystallization	trigonal crystal

When buying a phantom quartz, check that its distinctive characteristics are clearly visible.

Prase

History and legend

The name is derived from the Greek *prasinos* and means "leek-green." According to tradition, prase was used more as a healing and protective stone than as a gemstone. The healing properties of prase were already known in antiquity. Apollo's temple in Delphi was built mostly of precious prase in order to create inner calm for the priests and help them make balanced judgements. In the Middle Ages the stone was used to treat eye complaints.

Healing properties

Prase calms down hot-tempered people.

Prase can alleviate pain, muscle tension, and energy blockages. But it also has blood-staunching properties and promotes the healing of wounds. In addition, it improves blood circulation and is therefore the perfect remedy for cold hands and feet. Green prase has calming, settling properties and is therefore recommended

for those prone to anger because it promotes self-control and cools hot tempers.

Magical properties
Since time immemorial, green prase has symbolized inner peace and reflection and self-reflection.

Chacra classification
It is strongest and most effective on the heart chacra.

Star sign
Not linked to any particular star sign.

Application and care
Prase is discharged once a week under running warm water and charged in the sun among tumbled hematite stones.

Prase is also known as emerald quartz.

Where found	USA, Australia, South Africa
Color(s)	the stone comes in various shades of green, sometimes with black inclusions
Chemical composition	$SiO_2 + Ca_2 (Mg, Fe)_5 [(OH, F)/Si_4O_{11}]_2$
Hardness	7
Available forms	tumbled stone; it is also found in pendants and sliced for use with chakras
Crystallization	quartz with actinolite inclusions; trigonal crystal

Prase is frequently called African jade. This is very misleading because it has nothing in common with jade except for its green color. It belongs to the quartz family.

Pyrite

History and legend

The name is derived from the Greek *pyros*, meaning "fire," because the stone produces sparks when it is hit. In the Stone Age it was used to make fire. Being a "firestone," it was attributed magic properties in legends and mythology.

In the Middle Ages the alchemists believed that pyrite could be turned into gold.

Healing properties

Pyrite was highly valued as a healing stone in antiquity.

Pyrite is a powerful healing stone that is used in the treatment of bronchial problems. It is also used as remedy for lung infections. Stammering, cramp-like twitching and spasms in the upper body can be alleviated by regularly wearing a pyrite necklace. Pyrite removes mental blocks and reduces anxiety. It is therefore recommended as a touchstone during examinations.

Magical properties

Pyrite is a symbol of resolution. With this stone all problems can be solved.

Chacra classification

Pyrite works on the navel and throat chakras.

Star sign

Because of its magical properties, pyrite works well for all star signs.

Application and care

Pyrite should only be cleansed, discharged and recharged in dry sea salt. It needs the sun to develop its full sparkle. Never let it come into contact with water!

Related stones

Gold and silver shimmering pyrite sun is only found embedded in slate in the coal mines of Illinois. Unlike pyrite, it also contains organic substances. It should be discharged among tumbled hematite stones and recharged among rock crystals.

Pyrite sun is one of the strongest energy stones.

Where found	Sweden, USA, Mexico, Peru, Chile, Australia; the most beautiful pyrites come from the Isle of Elba
Color(s)	silver, brass yellow to golden
Chemical composition	FeS_2 + Co, Ni, Sb + (Ag, Au, Cu, Zn)
Hardness	6 to 6.5
Available forms	found naturally as stones for placing or laying on the body; especially beautiful crystals are roughly cut for use in jewelry
Crystallization	cubic crystals composed of iron sulfide; spherical and bulbous pyrites also exist; it is found in large quantities, mainly in coal mines and near clay workings

Pyrite sun has a calming effect on the vegetative nerve centre. It strengthens the liver, gall bladder and intestines, and reduces gastric acid and menstrual pain.

Rainbow jasper

History and legend
The Chinese have valued rainbow jasper as a powerful healing stone for thousands of years. The name jasper is derived from the Greek word *jaspis* meaning "speckled" or "mottled."

Healing properties
Rainbow jasper regulates glandular functions and consequently the production of hormones. In addition, it regulates the secretion of sweat and sebum.

Psychologically, it makes sensitive people stronger. Above all, it helps them to ward off attacks by resentful, malevolent people. It helps people prepare for decisive moments and great opportunities.

The reddish and yellowish to beige rainbow jasper is a quartz.

Magical properties
Rainbow jasper sharpens the intellect and thought processes.

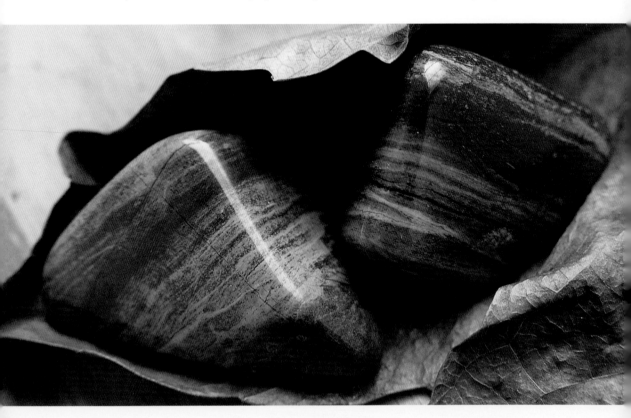

Chakra classification
The power of rainbow jasper is particularly effective on the sacral chakra.

Star sign
Not linked to any sign in particular.

Application and care
Cleanse and discharge jasper once or twice a month under warm running water. Recharge among other rock crystals with other jasper stones.

Related stones
Brown snake jasper has anti-bacterial properties and protects against infection. It has positive effects on the liver and regulates cholesterol levels. Psychologically, it encourages the link between mind and soul. It provides the will to survive and the necessary strength and endurance in difficult situations.

Snake jasper is brown with snake-like inclusions.

Where found	China, Australia
Color(s)	beige to reddish
Chemical composition	SiO_2
Hardness	7
Available forms	tumbled stone, touchstone, pendant
Crystallization	trigonal crystal

Snake jasper works on all the chakras. It must be cleansed once a month under warm running water and charged in the sun or among rock crystals.

Rainbow obsidian

History and legend
The Mexican Indians worshipped rainbow obsidian as the sanctuary of their gods. They believed that the gods inhabited rainbow obsidian when they visited the earth.

Healing properties
Rainbow obsidian regulates glandular functions and has a powerful effect on the thyroid gland, ovaries, pancreas, adrenal and pituitary glands. In addition, it strengthens and controls the nervous system. The stone is used in the treatment of various kinds of addiction. Rainbow obsidian strengthens the wearer's mental powers and identifies weaknesses.

Chakra classification
Rainbow obsidian can be used on all chakras.

Rainbow obsidian takes its name from the rainbow-like play of its colors.

Star sign
Not linked to any particular star sign.

Application and care
Discharge the stone regularly under warm running water. Recharge it by placing it in the sun or leaving it overnight among rock crystals.

Related stones
The snowflake obsidian also belongs to the family of obsidians. It is available as a tumbled stone, touchstone, pendant, necklace, sphere, pyramid, or chakra disk. It is particularly suited for laying on the secondary chakras. The black shiny snowflake obsidian has a snowflake-like pattern. It can raise the blood pressure and is therefore an excellent remedy against cold feet. Psychologically, it sharpens the possessor's view of his own personality. While doing so, it helps him achieve his hidden potential. It promotes intuition and gives him better insight into his own shortcomings. In addition, it protects him against negative influences of all kinds. The snowflake obsidian is the stone for those born under the sign of Libra. It is found mainly in Mexico and also in Millard County, Utah.

The amorphous stone is available in many forms, including tumbled stone and touchstone. It is also used as jewelry in the form of pendants, spheres, chakra disks, and pyramids.

Snowflake obsidian is the stone for all Libras.

Snowflake obsidian stimulates the circulation, strengthens the body's defences, combats allergies, and alleviates skin rashes. It can raise blood pressure, promote intuition, and protect against negative influences.

Where found	in volcanic regions
Color(s)	gray-black, colorful gleam
Chemical composition	$SiO_2 + Fe_2O_3 + H_2O + Al, C, Ca, Fe, K, Na$
Hardness	5.5
Available forms	sphere, lens-shaped, egg-shaped, cabochon
Crystallization	amorphous stone

Rhodochrosite

History and legend
The name is derived from the Greek *rhodochrosis* ("pink colored").
Native Americans used to offer the stone as a token of love, and
it was also worshipped as a holy stone.

Healing properties
It stabilizes the blood pressure and circulation and is used in the
treatment of hardening and narrowing arteries. That is why it is a
good remedy against chronic migraines, but the treatment must be
over a long period. In cases of acute attacks, a stone is placed on
the site of the pain at the back of the head and left until the pain
has abated.

The Indians worshipped rhodochrosite as the stone of love and the heart.

  Psychologically rhodochrosite helps the wearer to achieve self-
knowledge and protects him against slander.It is also useful in
reducing stress.

Magical properties
Rhodochrosite symbolizes openness. It awakens all-embracing love that is not limited to one person.

Chakra classification
Rhodochrosite works most strongly on the heart and navel chakras.

Star sign
Rhodochrosite is linked to Taurus.

Application and care
After each healing session, the stone must be briefly discharged under running water. Recharge the stone among rock crystals rather than in the sun. If you notice that the stone is becoming cloudy or discolored, wear it on your body until it returns to its normal color.

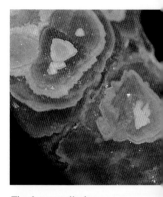

The Incas called rhodochrosite "Inca rose."

Where found	in many mining regions throughout the world, but usually in small crystals; large ones come from Peru and Colorado
Color(s)	pink, pink with partial white stripes
Chemical composition	$MnCO_3$ + Ca, Fe, Zn
Hardness	4 to 4.5
Available forms	polished for laying on the body or as a touchstone; cut as jewelry
Crystalli-zation	it is found as a trigonal crystal carbonate that is found in manganese mines as stalagmites or in cavities

Rhodochrosite has a detoxifying effect on the metabolism. Because of its cleansing properties it is a good remedy for skin problems such as spots and acne.

Rhodonite

History and legend
The word is derived from the Greek word *rhodon*, meaning "rose."
In antiquity rhodonite was given to travelers as a protective stone.
It was said to warn them of imminent danger by causing the heart-
beat to accelerate suddenly.

Healing properties
Rhodonite can improve cardiac deficiencies at an early stage and
tone up the respiratory tract and the lungs. It has a stimulating
effect on sexuality. It strengthens the possessor's immune system
and protects him against allergies. It also staves off primeval fears
and phobias. Rhodonite is helpful in keeping a clear, calm mind in
tense situations and in coping with changing circumstances such
as separations, a new job, a move or a long journey. It is helpful
during examinations and prevents mental blocks.

*Rhodonite is the
traveler's stone.*

Magical properties

Rhodonite symbolizes self-realization. It is known as the first-aid stone and is recognised as a beneficial travel companion. Pink rhodonite with its dark or black inclusions protects against all kinds of anxieties.

Chakra classification

Rhodonite is most effective on the heart and sacral chakras.

Star sign

Rhodonite is linked to Taurus.

Application and care

Rhodonite should be discharged every two weeks under running water and then recharged by being placed in the sun for a few hours.

Rhodonite and rhodochrosite both protect against anxieties and fears.

Where found	South Africa, Australia, China, USA, Mexico; also throughout the region of the Urals
Color(s)	pink with dark inclusions
Chemical composition	$CaMn_4 [Si_5O_{15}]$ + Al, Ca, Fe, K, Li, Na
Hardness	5.5 to 6.5
Available forms	polished and cut as a gemstone for jewelry
Crystallization	it is normally created by metamorphosis in magnanese ore mines where it forms chain silicate triclinic crystals, with black flecks formed by inclusions of manganese dioxide

If rhodonite is used to combat fear of exams, wearing a rhodonite necklace made with stones without black inclusions is recommended. Such stones are particularly powerful.

Rock crystal

History and legend

From antiquity until the Middle Ages, rock crystal was thought to be petrified ice (Greek: *krystallos*). Mountain people believed that gods and spirits lived in palaces made from rock crystal. They also believed that it quenched thirst. Nero used to drink his wine from rock crystal goblets, and the Emperor Augustus dedicated what was the then largest stone known to man to a divinity. Today, Native Americans still put this "holy stone" in every new-born baby's cradle.

Healing properties

Rock crystal is the ideal stone for meditation.

Applied to the body, rock crystal can alleviate pain and reduce fever. It has an invigorating effect, especially on weakened intervertebral disks. It helps treat stomach, bowel, and heart problems. Its positive energy removes mental blocks and promotes a sense of justice. Crystal spheres held in the hand have a calming effect.

Magical properties

Buddhists use this stone to achieve enlightenment. From time immemorial the crystal ball used by clairvoyants has been made of rock crystal.

Chakra classification

Rock crystal has an enlightening effect on all chakras. It is a particularly good combination stone because it opens up all chakras for relaxation. In addition it reduces the strength of stones that are too powerful during meditation.

Star sign

This stone is associated with Leo, Gemini and Capricorn.

Application and care

As a geode in the room, rock crystal reinforces the effect of other stones. The larger the stone the more power it develops. Always store rock crystal necklaces overnight in a bowl of dry tumbled hematite stones. Rock crystal should be cleansed once or twice a month under running water and recharged in the sun.

The pyramidal shape of a rock crystal contains bundled energy.

Rock crystal can revive numb, paralyzed parts of the body. With its coolness it can stop minor bleeding and reduce blisters caused by burns.

Where found	worldwide, particularly in the Alps, Brazil and USA (Arkansas)
Color(s)	clear to white and transparent
Chemical composition	SiO_2
Hardness	7
Available forms	small crystal as a pendant; little pieces as a touchstone; polished or cut as jewelry; rough stone in groups for laying on the body
Crystallization	this quartz is made from pure silicon oxide and forms trigonal crystals; these crystals are male (pointed on top) and female (smooth on top)

Rock salt

History and legend
Salt has brought great wealth to merchants in the past; salt roads were the first great trade routes in Europe. It was along these routes that salt was transported from where it was mined to the various towns and cities. The duties and rights of ways on these important trade routes were a lucrative source of income for both secular and ecclesiastical authorities.

Healing properties
Rock salt is mined in salt mines that may be as deep as 300 feet.

Rock salt stimulates the metabolism and blood circulation, especially when a glass of salt water is drunk first thing in the morning. Salt is necessary to maintain the fluid balance in the body. Salt baths brighten up the skin and hair and are very effective in cases of severe skin diseases such as neurodermitis. However, too much salt can be damaging.

Magical properties

Rock salt, whose mineral name is halite, has been used for seasoning food for thousands of years.

Chakra classification

Rock salt is not suitable for meditation and is only used for medicinal purposes.

Star sign

Not linked to any sign in particular.

Application and care

Rinse in water just before using (but only very briefly!). Store in dry conditions. In contrast to sea salt, rock salt is very pure and has a high concentration of minerals and trace elements. It has a cubic crystal structure and is found in several colors.

Humans, animals, and plants all need salt to survive.

Also known as halite, rock salt is a compound of sodium and chlorine. It frequently crystallises in the form of cubes.

Where found	USA, former Soviet Union, Germany and China
Color(s)	colorless, pink, bluish; rock salt is transparent
Chemical composition	NaCl
Hardness	2
Available forms	when buying in the supermaket, check carefully to avoid the wrong salt; rock salt contains no additional chemicals
Crystallization	sodium chloride composition; cubic crystal

Rose quartz

History and lgend

According to legend, Eros brought rose quartz to the earth in the hope that its beautiful color would arouse love and desire among people. It has been perceived as an important fertility stone for many centuries, as it still is today. Since the Middle Ages, rose quartz has been given as a love charm to young girls.

Healing properties

Rose quartz is found naturally as a piece of quartz the size of a fist. It is the most effective stone against damaging radiation: placed next to the computer it can prevent headaches and eye fatigue, while placed next to the bed it is effective against earth radiation and water radiation, thus improving the quality of sleep. It is important to discharge the stone once a week under running water. Rose quartz stimulates the circulation and thus increases

The finest specimens of rose quartz with the most intense colors come from Madagascar.

sexuality and fertility. It relieves pain associated with shingles and has a refreshing effect. Psychologically, rose quartz strengthens friendships, combats lovesickness and opens the mind to beautiful things.

Magical properties
Rose quartz symbolizes trust and brotherly love. It is also very helpful in affairs of the heart.

Chakra classification
Rose quartz is most effective on the heart chakra.

Star sign
Rose quartz is linked with Taurus and, as a secondary stone, Libra.

Application and care
Rose quartz can manifest its powerful energy even when simply placed in a room as a raw stone. It is discharged under running water or among tumbled hematite stones. It is best recharged overnight in an amethyst geode.

Rose quartz owes its color to the presence of manganese and iron-rutile needles.

Rose quartz has a wide range of healing properties. It has a beneficial effect on the heart, blood and circulation. A long rose quartz necklace alleviates pain in the region of the heart and lovesickness.

Where found	Madagascar, Brazil, USA, Austria
Color(s)	pink, translucent
Chemical composition	SiO_2 + Al, Fe, Na, Ti + (Ca, Mg, Mn)
Hardness	7
Available forms	polished for laying on the body and as a touchstone; fist-sized rough mineral for use as an energy stone; cut as a gemstone for jewelry
Crystallization	trigonal quartz oxide crystal; the color comes from manganese and fine needles of rutile-iron; these needles are concentrically arranged so that when cut in a certain way a star is revealed

Ruby

History and legnd

The name comes from the Latin *rubeus* meaning "red." Because of its beauty and rarity, the Greeks called it the mother of all gem-stones. Aristotle wrote: "One of them is red like blood and is called *rubinus*. This is the best one of all." The Romans called it "a flower among stones." It is said that the ruby combines Eros, sensual love, and Agape, spiritual love, and is therefore divine love in crystal-lized form. In the Middle Ages ruby was used as protection against the plague. If the color became darker, the wearer fled to another place in order to protect himself against infection, only returning home when the stone became lighter again.

Ruby is blood red; it is often marked with a star and is then known as star ruby.

Healing properties

Ruby promotes sexual energy when it is moved to and fro over the genital area. It strengthens the body's immune system against

infectious diseases, fortifies the heart and circulation, and combats low blood pressure. Ruby helps cure eye infections even when worn as jewelry.

Psychologically, ruby is the good-luck stone of love, encouraging sensitivity in a relationship.

Magical properties
Red ruby symbolizes love and passion. The stone is associated with vitality and strong feelings.

Chakra classification
It works best on the root and heart chakras.

Star sign
Ruby is linked to Aries.

Application and care
Ruby should be discharged twice every month under running water and recharged in sunlight for two hours.

After diamond, ruby and sapphire are the hardest gemstones.

Where found	Siberia, Thailand, India, Myanmar, Siam, Sri Lanka, Brazil
Color(s)	red, rarely translucent
Chemical composition	Al_2O_3 + Cr
Hardness	9
Available forms	cut as jewelry or for laying on the body
Crystallization	it belongs to the corundum family; trigonal crystallized aluminum oxide; the color comes from traces of chromium; occasionally concentric rutile needles enable the stone to be cut as a star ruby

Ruby or garnet is thought to have been the legendary carbuncle forming the ruby bowl of the Holy Grail, containing a few drops of the blood of Christ.

Rutilated quartz

History and legend
Rutilated quartz used to be known as "the hair of Venus" or sagenite. It is said to contain the light of the sun and is helpful in lifting depression and alleviating coughing.

Healing properties
Rutilated quartz reduces coughing caused by bronchitis or asthma. It has a beneficial effect on the lungs, bronchial tubes and respiratory tract, combating inflammation. It also regulates the nervous system and strengthens the immune system.

Rutilated quartz has a calming effect on the psyche and promotes healthy sleep. It stimulates the wearer's self-healing powers and removes mental blocks. If he indulges in negative thoughts, it will help him discover the truth. As a result, it makes it possible for him to bring about changes.

For thousands of years rutilated quartz has been valued as a protective and truth stone.

Magical properties
Rutilated quartz symbolizes truth.

Chakra classification
Rutilated quartz is most effective on the navel and throat chakras.

Star sign
Not associated with any particular star sign.

Application and care
Cleanse rutilated quartz once or twice a month under running water and charge it in the sun or among rock crystals.

The more golden the needle-like rutile inclusions, the stronger the properties of the stone.

Where found	Brazil, Australia, USA; the stone is also found in the region of the Alps
Color(s)	transparent with needle-shaped reddish inclusions
Chemical composition	$SiO_2 + TiO_2$
Hardness	7
Available forms	rough stone, crystal, touchstone, tumbled stone; as a jewelry stone, often as a pendant; rutilated quartz combines well with other stones
Crystallization	trigonal crystal

Transparent rutilated quartz with its characteristic reddish, brown or golden inclusions is a rock crystal. The colored needles are rutile crystals that have formed within the crystal.

Sapphire

History and legend
The Bible likens sapphire to the blue of the sky. The prophet Ezekiel wrote: "Then I looked, and, behold, in the firmament that was above the head of the cherubim there appeared over them as it were a sapphire stone, as the appearance of the likeness of a throne." In Revelation, sapphire is named as one of the foundation stones of New Jerusalem. Sapphire is said to have received its protective power from Saturn and it was highly regarded in antiquity by kings and emperors. In 200 A.D., Damigeron wrote: "Sapphire has been blessed with great honor by the gods, kings wear it round their neck because it is the most powerful protective stone."

The name "sapphire" is derived from the Sanskrit sani.

Healing properties
Sapphire is the most effective healing stone for the nervous system. It regulates the function of the thyroid gland and is therefore

a useful remedy for lack of appetite and nervous heart trouble. Psychologically, it strengthens the wearer's willpower and gives him the strength to get better.

Magical properties
Sapphire symbolizes faith. Its blue color represents the sky as well as loyalty and friendship.

Chakra classification
Sapphire is most effective on the forehead chakra, the third eye.

Star sign
Blue sapphire is linked to Pisces, light-blue sapphire to Taurus, yellow sapphire to Gemini and star sapphire to Libra.

Application and care
Sapphire should discharged and at the same time recharged in sea salt, avoiding exposure to sunlight if possible.

A hot sapphire bath is very beneficial for sufferers from rheumatism.

Where found	Sri Lanka, Myanmar, northern India, Australia, Brazil, North America
Color(s)	usually blue, also green, yellow and purple-black
Chemical composition	Al_2O_3 + Fe, Ti
Hardness	9
Available forms	cut as jewelry, jewelry stone for laying on the body
Crystallization	sapphire is an aluminum oxide and belongs to the very hard corundum family; it forms trigonal crystals in slate, marble, and gneiss; traces of metals give it various colors; the celebrated blue sapphire owes its color to iron and titanium

Magical powers have been ascribed to this precious stone. Hildegard von Bingen is said to have used it successfully in treating people possessed by the devil.

Sard

History and legend

The name is said to be derived from the ancient city of Sardes in Asia Minor. The Greeks and Romans called it the "stone of fire." The Bible mentions sard in Revelation, although sard and carnelian are often confused. Sard tended to be used as a cult stone rather than as a gemstone.

Healing properties

Sard is one of the most important healing stones. It is used to treat tumors, ulcers and myomas. The regular drinking of sard water is believed to alleviate liver and gall bladder problems. As the "stone of fire" sard is an excellent remedy for arthritis, gout, and rheumatism. In this case it is usually applied to the site of the pain.

Psychologically, it strengthens friendships and partnerships and reduces egotism and fanaticism. It sharpens the mind and

Hildegard von Bingen believed that sard was one of the most powerful healing stones.

encourages openness with one's fellow human beings. It is a good stone to counteract selfishness and introversion.

Magical properties
Sard symbolizes justice. It has always been used predominantly as a cult and healing stone rather than as a gemstone.

Chakra classification
Sard works best on the root chakra.

Star sign
Sard is linked to Scorpio.

Application and care
Discharge in a bowl of water and tumbled hematite stones. Recharge the stone in the hot midday sun.

In Brazil pieces as large as a human head have been found.

Where found	all over Brazil, where large pieces are found; elsewhere: India, Madagascar, Australia, South-West Africa, and also Germany
Color(s)	red to brownish in a variety of shades
Chemical composition	SiO_2 + Fe
Hardness	7
Available forms	it is usually employed only as a touchstone
Crystallization	it is a member of the chalcedony quartz family, a silicon oxide that is often crystallized with sardonyx; this is however black with white, streaky inclusions; trigonal crystal

Reddish-brown sard is a chalcedony agate and a member of the quartz family. Its unmistakable color is formed by the concentration of various limonite and iron oxides.

Sardonyx

History and legend

The name of this stone is a combination of the names of two healing stones, sard and onyx. The healing and protective properties of sardonyx were known in antiquity. It is the stone of abundance, virtue and eloquence. In the Book of Revelation it is described as one of the twelve foundation stones of the walls of the New Jerusalem, and as one of the twelve stones in the cuirass worn by the High Priest that made him "glow through and through." Hildegard von Bingen used it as a remedy against fever and to calm irascible tempers.

The white stripes give this dark-colored onyx its distinctive appearance.

Healing properties

Sardonyx is the stone of the senses. It improves sensory perception and strengthens the parasympathetic nervous system. It reinforces the immune system by stimulating the flow of body fluids.

Sardonyx is particularly effective in preventing bronchitis and infections of the respiratory tract. Back problems and liver disorders can also be alleviated by the application of sardonyx to the affected organs.Sardonyx sharpens the mind. It helps the wearer confront the world with open eyes and not to get lost in dreams and wishful thinking. It encourages optimism and confidence in the wearer and helps bereaved people see the positive side of life again.

Chakra classification
Sardonyx is most effective on the throat chakra but it also works on the forehead and root chakras.

Star sign
Sardonyx encourages the sense of reality in Capricorns and also helps Aries to distinguish what is essential.

Application and care
Sardonyx is discharged once a week either under running water or overnight in a bowl of tumbled hematite stones. It is charged by being placed in sunlight for several hours.

Beautifully grained, black and white striped sardonyx is very rare.

This variety of chalcedony, a member of the quartz family, is found mainly in Brazil.

Where found	China, India, South-West Africa, Australia, Brazil and Uruguay
Color(s)	black and white, banded with reddish brown
Chemical composition	SiO_2 + C + Fe, O, OH
Hardness	6.5 to 7
Available forms	tumbled stone, polished disks or worked as a necklace
Crystallization	sardonyx is a kind of chalcedony that originated in rock cavities; trigonal crystal

Serpentine

History and legend

Serpentine was used by the ancient Romans as a protective stone against the powers of darkness. According to legend, beakers made from serpentine would shatter if they came into contact with poison. Bowls and vessels were often made of serpentine. In the Middle Ages medicine was kept in serpentine containers because this increased its healing powers and made it last longer. In China aphrodisiacs, healing, and magic potions were drunk from specially shaped serpentine beakers. Here, as in ancient civilizations of America, serpentine was considered a guardian of vital energy and a protector of the soul against invisible powers.

The greenish, shiny serpentine is a magnesium silicate.

Healing properties

Serpentine can be used to treat a wide range of disorders. It is beneficial for cardiac irregularities, kidney disorders, stomach

and bowel trouble, and menstrual problems. It evens out mood swings and calms the wearer in stressful, hectic situations.

Magical properties
In ancient civilizations, serpentine was seen as a talisman. It was said to protect against demonic powers and promote fertility. It is still used to protect against snake bites, poison, and magic spells. In China and India it is often incorporated in altars, temple decorations and carvings. It is a protective stone that brings peace.

Chakra classification
Serpentine is particularly powerful on the heart and sacral chakras.

Star sign
Not linked to any particular star sign.

Application and care
Serpentine is discharged under warm running water and charged overnight in water with rock crystals, but only for a few hours if charged in sunlight. It is important that it should not become too hot.

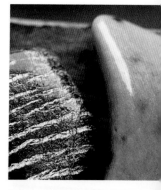

When used in meditation, serpentine should be reinforced by jade or chrysoprase.

In the nineteenth century people became aware of the fire-resistant qualities of serpentine. As a result it was used in many materials and fabrics.

Where found	South-West Africa, China, India, USA, also Italy
Color(s)	yellowish, greenish, brown, oily sheen
Chemical composition	$Mg_6 [(OH)_{10} / Si_4O_{10}] + Al, Cr, Fe, Mn, Ni$
Hardness	3 to 4
Available forms	as a rough stone, tumbled stone and touchstone; also a jewelry stone as beads in necklaces and pendants
Crystallization	amorphous stone

Silver

History and legend

The role played by silver in ancient civilizations is similar to that played by gold. Until the eighteenth century silver was considered almost as valuable as gold.

Silver jewelry was produced as early as the fourth millennium B.C. Saxony was for a long time the main supplier of silver and it became very rich as a result. After the discovery of the Americas by the Europeans so much silver was mined in the United States and Mexico that the price and the value attached to silver fell sharply. Today the largest deposits of silver are found in Mexico, Australia and the former Soviet Union. Silver is a precious metal, not a mineral.

Silver is most effective when combined with a healing stone.

Healing properties

Silver transmits and intensifies the power of healing stones so that when they are set in silver they become even more powerful.

Silver regulates the bodily fluids and counteracts hyperacidity. Combined with a healing stone, silver promotes weight loss. Nausea, painful joints, headaches, and migraine can be alleviated with silver together with the appropriate healing stones. Psychologically, silver has a calming effect on irritable people and encourages inner peace.

Silver promotes self-confidence and removes inhibitions.

Magical properties
Like gold, silver symbolizes wealth and prosperity, and is widely used in coinage. Those prone to outbursts of anger and rudeness can be pacified by silver.

Chakra classification
Silver works well on all chakras.

Star sign
Not linked to any particular star sign.

Application and care
Silver increases the power of most healing stones, especially turquoise and coral, so use silver to this effect.

Silver increases the power of weaker stones and reduces the power of very strong ones. If a healing stone is too weak or too powerful for you, use it in combination with silver.

Where found	Australia, Mexico, former Soviet Union
Color(s)	shiny silver
Chemical composition	Ag
Hardness	2.5 to 3
Available forms	industrial; table silver, objects of art, jewelry
Crystallization	it is a soft precious metal, not a mineral

Smoky quartz

History and legend

In antiquity smoky quartz was used as a protective stone. It was said to warn fighting soldiers of danger by turning darker. Because of the stone's dark color, the ancient Romans considered it a mourning stone that helped overcome grief. The most beautiful smoky quartz comes from Brazil, the United States, Australia, and the Alps. In Alpine countries, rosaries and crucifixes are made from smoky quartz with its protective properties.

Healing properties

Smoky quartz crystals that are almost completely black are known as morion quartz.

It is a stone that strengthens the supporting and connective tissue as well as the muscles. It stabilizes the joints and stimulates fertility by activating the production of the sexual glands. If a couple wishes to have children both partners should drink smoky quartz water every morning over a long period.

Smoky quartz also brings inner calm to its possessor. A smoky quartz should be held in each hand in stressful situations. Uncut stones are also effective. They help give renewed strength to overcome grief.

Magical properties
Smoky quartz stands for facing life, giving strength and motivation to meet new challenges.

Chakra classification
Smoky quartz works best on the sacral chakra.

Star sign
Smoky quartz is linked to Libra.

Application and care
Smoky quartz should be discharged once a month under warm running water and charged overnight among rock crystals.

Smoky quartz is a beneficial stone for those in mourning.

Smoky quartz is a translucent smoky-brown to black rock crystal. There is also radiant smoky quartz that comes from Arkansas but these are less powerful as healing stones.

Where found	all over the world
Color(s)	red-brown to solid black, translucent; very dark varieties are called morion
Chemical composition	SiO_2 + (Al, Li, Na)
Hardness	7
Available forms	often in geodes for placing on the body, otherwise polished or cut
Crystallization	silicon oxide trigonal crystals usually in geodes; the color is caused by aluminum, lithium and radioactive radiation

Soapstone

History and legend

Soapstone was known by 4000 B.C. and is still used for all kinds of carvings because the soft stone is easy to work. The well-known pipes of peace used by American Indian tribes were almost all made of soapstone. Since time immemorial it has been known that ground soapstone made into a paste has a rejuvenating and regenerating effect on the skin. Hildegard von Bingen described these properties extensively in her works. Today soapstone is used in many cosmetics.

Healing properties

Soapstone is very soft and therefore very easy to carve.

Soapstone is helpful in the treatment of many skin problems. Red patches and itchy skin can be alleviated by applying soapstone to the affected places. Chronic skin problems or larger affected areas such as those caused by acne, sunburn or allergies can be

treated by applying soapstone ointment. Powdered soapstone helps prevent sweaty hands and gives relief to people with a tendency to sweat heavily. Soapstone helps young people to develop their own personality. In addition, it gives the wearer a sense of ambition at school and at work.

Magical properties
Because soapstone is a very soft material it teaches sensitive people how to deal with the world around them.

Chakra classification
Soapstone is not a meditation stone.

Star sign
Not linked to any particularly sign.

Application and care
It is ground to make essences or bath salts. If a soapstone seems a bit dull, bury it in the ground for a few days in order to build up its energy again.

Soapstone is found everywhere in the world.

Where found	all over the world
Color(s)	white, gray, pink, red, yellow and greenish
Chemical composition	$Mg_3 [(OH)_2 / Si_4O_{10}]$
Hardness	1
Available forms	powdered, or as pieces
Crystallization	monoclinic crystal

Since time immemorial soapstone has been ground to make powder and ointment as a skin care or healing product.

Sodalite

History and legend

The name is derived from two Greek words *soda* (salt) and *lithos* (stone) because it is a stone that contains a lot of salt. Since antiquity sodalite has been known as the stone of artists, singers, painters and sculptors because it is believed to promote inspiration and creativity while also providing protection. It was not used in the Middle Ages but has been rediscovered in modern times and is now a popular gemstone and healing stone.

Healing properties

Sodalite is an excellent stone for reducing high blood pressure if always carried on the person. Necklaces of sodalite beads that hang down as far as the heart area will increase its hypotensive properties. It also has a calming, regulatory effect on the thyroid gland, the vegetative nervous system and all glandular functions.

Sodalite has inclusions of calcium, salt, and manganese.

Sodalite water, drunk every day first thing in the morning, is very effective against diabetes. Sodalite promotes spiritual harmony and is a source of artistic inspiration. It is also an ideal stone for calming hot-tempered people.

Magical properties

Blue sodalite symbolizes self-confidence and loyalty. In ancient Greece artists and singers used to carry sodalite. It was believed to develop the possessor's musical skills.

Chakra classification

Sodalite is most effective on the forehead chakra.

Star sign

Sodalite is especially recommended for Sagittarius.

Applications and care

In order to benefit from the stone's energy, it must be worn or carried around as a touchstone over a long period. It should be discharged under running water weekly, or whenever the stone becomes cloudy or changes color, and charged again in a bowl of water together with rock crystal.

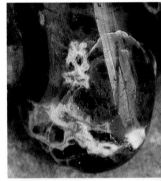

Sodalite cannot store the warmth of sunlight.

Dark blue sodalite is a quartz sodium-calcium compound. It can be identified by the white inclusions of calcium.

Where found	Brazil, South-West Africa, China
Color(s)	dark blue
Chemical composition	$Na_8 [Cl_2/(AlSiO_4)_6]$ + Be, K, Mg
Hardness	5 to 6
Available forms	polished as a touchstone and for laying on the body, cut as a jewelry stone
Crystallization	a sodium-quartz cubic crystal of frame silicate form; white markings caused by calcium inclusions

Sphalerite

History and legend

Sphalerite, also called zinc blende, has been mined since the Middle Ages. But no mention of its healing properties dates from that time.

Healing properties

Since there is no mention of the healing properties of sphalerite in ancient documents, its use is guided by recent experiences. Sphalerite promotes the erotic relationship between two people. If the relationship has cooled down a little sphalerite will revive it. It also strengthens brain functions and is an effective treatment for prostate problems. Its high content of trace elements encourages growth. It also speeds up the healing process in skin disorders such as eczema and acne.

Sphalerite is a good source of energy in cases of mental exhaus-

Sphalerite has a reputation as a strongly erotic stone.

tion, giving its possessor confidence when he feels despondent and stopping him from brooding. This enables him to switch gears, to let go and find peace.

Chakra classification
Sphalerite is particularly effective on the root chakra.

Star sign
Not linked to any star sign in particular.

Application and care
Discharge sphalerite once a month under warm running water. Recharge by placing among rock crystals overnight.

Sphalerite's healing properties are due to the presence of trace elements.

Where found	Spain, former Yugoslavia, Peru, Russia, Canada
Color(s)	various shades: blackish-brown, brown, yellow, orange
Chemical composition	(Zn, Fe) S
Hardness	3.5 to 4
Available forms	usually found as a rough stone or crystal in zinc blende; occasionally worked for use in jewelry
Crystallization	cubic crystal, often tetrahedral, striped, twinned

A compound of zinc and sulfur, sphalerite can be recognized by its uneven sparkling surface. It is often brightly colored and translucent when held against the light.

Spinel

History and legend

Until about one hundred and fifty years ago spinel was often confused with ruby or sapphire, and supposed rubies or sapphires can still be found in the treasure chambers of many rulers. The melting point of spinel is an incredible 2135 °C, an amazingly high temperature.

Healing properties

Spinel has a calming effect on all kinds of inflammations. Even neuritis and its symptoms can benefit from it. Stomach ulcers and hyperpepsia can be successfully treated by drinking spinel water. Torn muscles heal more quickly with spinel. The stone speeds the recovery of all diseases associated with movement, including problems with muscles, joints, and bones.

It is a stone of calm, loyalty and meditation. It helps in stressful

Spinel is only occasionally found in the form of large crystals.

situations and reduces anxiety. It also helps in crises such as changing one's job, separation or divorce. Spinel strengthens the wearer and increases his powers of self-healing. This makes it possible to protect himself from the troublesome influence of others.

Magical properties
Spinel symbolizes purposefulness. It helps the wearer recognize what is right for him and gives him the energy to act accordingly.

Chakra classification
Red spinel is most effective on the root chakra, blue spinel on the forehead chakra, and violet spinel on the crown chakra.

Star sign
Dark blue spinel is linked to Sagittarius. Red spinel is very effective for Scorpio.

Application and care
Spinel should be discharged once a month under running water and recharged for a short time in sunlight.

Spinel is one of the most precious gemstones and is very rare.

The name spinel is derived from the Greek spinther, which means "sparkling." It was particularly valued as a gemstone and protective stone by the Greeks and Romans because of its sparkling colors.

Where found	Sweden, Afghanistan, USA, Sri Lanka
Color(s)	pink, red, violet, orange, blue, dark green, black, translucent
Chemical composition	$MgAl_2O_4$
Hardness	8
Available forms	cut and worked
Crystallization	cubic crystal octahedron of magnesium-aluminum oxide, very rare and usually only found as very small stones in metamorphic rocks in alluvial deposits

Staurolite

History and legend

The name staurolite is derived from the Greek words *stauros-lithos*, literally translateds "cross-stone." It is the ancient name of chiastolite. Many civilizations have regarded it as a good luck and protective stone, and Christians saw it as the connecting stone between heaven and earth. Staurolite usually has the form of a St Andrews cross, and very occasionally that of a traditional cross. Both shapes have a similar effect.

Healing properties

Staurolite protects children from cramp, brain tumors, and cerebral or spastic infantile paralysis. Staurolite can also help smokers give up smoking. Infectious diseases and fever can be alleviated by staurolite. The stone can be used successfully in the treatment of brain diseases and the central nervous system as

Staurolite is found in salt mines at depths of up to 300 feet.

well as headaches. In addition, it can prevent epileptic seizures and epilepsy that can lead to unconsciousness. Staurolite brings the wearer back to reality, especially those who are prone to exaggeration and megalomania. It also is helpful in the treatment of schizophrenia. It defuses stressful situations and lifts depression.

Chakra classification
Staurolite is most effective on the forehead chakra.

Star sign
Not linked to any sign in particular.

Application and care
Discharge the stone regularly once or twice a month under running warm water. Recharge overnight among clear rock crystals.

Staurolite is usually only found in the form of crystals.

Staurolite is a mostly brown, gray, or brown-gray stone that crystallizes in the shape of a cross. It is usually only obtainable in this characteristic crystal formation.

Where found	USA, France, Madagascar, Australia and Brazil
Color(s)	in various shades of gray and brown, such as reddish-brown, dark brown, yellow-brown, brownish-black, brownish-yellow
Chemical composition	$2FeO \cdot AlOOH \cdot 4Al_2[O/SiO_4]$
Hardness	7 to 7.5
Available forms	crystal
Crystallization	orthorhombic crystal

Sugilite

History and legend
Sugilite was named after the Japanese scientist Dr K. Sugi who discovered it in 1944. Those who are interested in the stone's magical associations believe that it highlights the destructive power of cosmic radiation, and that it is one of the final warnings to humanity of the end of the world.

Healing properties
Sugilite has a calming effect on the nervous system. It is said to alleviate pain and help in the treatment of epilepsy and disturbances of the nervous system. It is also thought that it can combat life-threatening diseases in people and animals, even at an advanced stage. Sugilite helps its possessor act logically and with determination in the face of unpleasant situations. It assists children who are having difficulty in learning to read and write.

Sugilite is one of the rarest discoveries of recent times.

Magical properties

Sugilite symbolizes self-control. It is said that it will warn people when the end of the world is imminent. Because the stone is found in Africa where mankind originated, many people believe that it has been drawn from the depths of the earth by the force of the planets in order to protect humanity against damaging cosmic radiation as well as against serious disorders such as megalomania.

Chakra classification

It is very effective on all the chakras.

Star sign

The stone is linked to Pisces and Libra.

Application and care

The stone must be discharged once a month among tumbled hematite stones. It does not need charging because it is so full of energy.

Lenticular and bead sugilite necklaces have the purest power.

Sugilite is a lilac, or often dark lilac, opaque mineral-rich silicon oxide. The stone is one of the most precious gemstones.

Where found	South Africa, Japan (very rare)
Color(s)	lilac, opaque
Chemical composition	$(K, Na)_2 / (Ti, Fe)_2 (Li, Al)_3 [Si_{12}O_{30}]$
Hardness	6.5 to 7
Available forms	polished as a touchstone or for laying on the body, as a sphere or pyramid; worked or cut as a gemstone for jewelry
Crystallization	it occurs in gaseous deposits of basic magma; hexagonal crystal

Sunstone

History and legend
Sunstone is dedicated to the Greek sun-god Helios because of its golden sparkle. The Greeks believed that sunstone protected the earth from disaster and kept the sun on its right course.

Healing properties
Sunstone promotes its wearer's self-healing powers. It stimulates the vegetative nervous system and ensures the harmonious functioning of all the organs. It is very helpful in cases of exhaustion caused by lack of sleep. It has an invigorating effect on the heart, back, eyes, and kidneys and is also very effective in cases of poor blood circulation.

Sunstone is an excellent remedy for disturbed sleep.

In addition, it has very positive effects on the psyche: sunstone promotes good humor, cheerfulness and good temper. It provides the necessary stamina and energy to undertake projects and tasks.

It gives self-confidence and helps its wearer to discover his own nature and live accordingly. It helps him to have a positive attitude towards his own life and to use his own strengths while allowing his sunny side to come to the fore. It lifts depression and helps him free himself from feelings of discrimination and failure as well as of images of an evil world. Sunstone increases the sense of self-esteem and self-confidence.

Sunstone water is an excellent treatment for gout.

Chakra classification
Sunstone is most effective on the sacral chakra.

Star sign
Not linked to any sign in particular.

Application and care
Sunstone should be cleansed and discharged once a month under running lukewarm water and recharged by being placed in sunlight for several hours.

Where found	USA, Canada, Madagascar, India, Norway
Color(s)	reddish-brown iridescent, translucent
Chemical composition	Na [AlSi$_3$O$_8$] + Fe
Hardness	6 to 6.5
Available forms	rough stone, tumbled stone, touchstone, pendant; very occasionally also used as a necklace
Crystallization	triclinic crystal

Traditional sunstone should not be confused with the sunstone known as aventurine, which belongs to the quartz family.

Sunstone (aventurine)

History and legend

Aventurine sunstone is a fiery energy stone. The Indians and Chinese believed that it promoted potency. When the stone arrived in Europe only the most prosperous members of society could afford it. Some Venetian glassmakers tried to produce the stone synthetically and in the process invented a glass that looked remarkably like sunstone. Inspired by the name of the stone they called this glass aventurine.

Healing properties

The stone's color is caused by the presence of very fine stripes of hematite and mica.

Aventurine sunstone is used in the treatment of stomach and bowel problems. It is particularly helpful with digestive disorders, flatulence, and stomachache. Bowel ulcers and inflammations of the intestinal wall also benefit from being treated with sunstone. The stone also has a positive effect on the wearer's psyche. It has a

soothing, pacifying effect on the soul and is therefore particularly suited for irascible, quick-tempered people.

Chakra classification

Sunstone should be used on the third chakra. Because of its influence on the navel chakra, it will help the wearer to achieve peace and contentment.

Star sign

Not associated with any particular star sign.

Application and care

Depending on the requirements, it should be cleansed once or twice a month under warm running water. It can be charged in sunlight, but be careful with darker stones in case their energy becomes too strong.

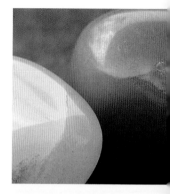

Sunstone can be used successfully with other healing stones.

Where found	India, Australia, Canada
Color(s)	orange-brown, orange-yellow, often with shimmering metallic inclusions
Chemical composition	SiO_2
Hardness	7
Available forms	rough stone, touchstone, pendant, necklace; it is also used in the form of a sphere or pyramid
Crystallization	trigonal crystal

The orange-brown or orange-yellow aventurine is a stone that promotes equilibrium and calmness. It drives away anger and reduces outbursts of rage.

Tiger's eye

History and legend
The stone takes its name from its resemblance to an eye. This appears when the brown inclusions are cut in a certain way, as is the case with cat's eye and falcon's eye. For about a hundred years it has been highly sought after and used in jewelry or for therapeutic purposes.

Healing properties
Tiger's eye is a particularly effective healing stone for bronchial problems when applied to the navel chakra. For acute bronchitis it is left overnight secured in place with a tape. Asthmatics should always carry a tiger's eye. It is also helpful in the case of headaches and migraines.

Tiger's eye is effective in treating any problems of the head.

Psychologically, tiger's eye is effective in lifting depression and promoting concentration.

Magical properties

The silky-shimmering, golden sparkling tiger's eye is a member of the quartz family. Its cat's eye effect is caused by hornblende fibers that all crystallize in the same direction. It symbolizes unity and leads to greater self-integration and autonomy.

Chakra classification

The tiger's eye is very effective on the navel chakra and solar plexus.

Star sign

Tiger's eye is associated with Virgo.

Application and care

Tiger's eye jewelry should only be worn for a few days because it stems the flow of energy. After being used for healing purposes it should be discharged under running water and then recharged in sunlight for a few hours.

The yellow cat's eye is a good stone for Scorpios.

Where found	South Africa, Western Australia, India, USA
Color(s)	shimmering golden-brown, with stripes
Chemical composition	SiO_2 + FeOOH
Hardness	6.5 to 7
Available forms	polished stone used as a touchstone or for laying on the body; worked or cut it is also used as a gemstone in jewelry
Crystallization	parallel rod-shaped quartz aggregate trigonal crystal with fibrous limonite (= brown iron) inclusions; formed by the further oxidation of falcon's eye through weathering

Cat's eye alleviates pain in the joints and bones and is helpful in the treatment of tendinitis and neuritis. It should be charged among rock crystals and a tiger's eye.

Topaz

History and legend

The name is derived either from the Arabic word *topazos* ("found") or the Indian *tapas* ("fire"). Topaz is unquestionably an ancient healing stone and gemstone. In antiquity it was linked to Jupiter and was therefore considered a symbol of the power of a ruler on whom it also bestowed wisdom. The royal crown of England is set with nearly five hundred topazes that were mined in the Erzgebirge ("Ore Mountains"). According to the Bible, topaz is one of the protective stones of the New Jerusalem. In ancient Mexico the stone was used in conflicts to ascertain the truth, in which event the stone would become slightly darker.

Healing properties

Topaz strengthens the nerves with its powerful energy.

Topaz stimulates the metabolism and digestion, heightening the tastebuds. According to ancient tradition, it staunches the flow of

blood. It promotes relaxation and eases tension. White topaz helps the wearer to take on new projects. Blue topaz promotes artistic inspiration. Yellow topaz counteracts bad moods and calms irritability caused by lack of sleep.

Magical properties
Topaz symbolizes the joy of life, Its wearer will take delight in the world and himself and embark on the path of self-realization.

Chakra classification
Gold topaz is effective on the navel and sacral chakras. White topaz works on all the chakras, while blue topaz works on the throat chakra.

Star sign
Gold topaz is linked to Virgo, pink to Leo and blue to Aquarius.

Application and care
Topaz should be cleansed under running water after each use and recharged again by being placed in sunlight for a few hours.

Topaz is translucent and is found in several colors ranging from white, blue, pink, and yellowish, as above, to orange.

Topazes are a family in their own right. The white or silver topaz is an aluminum-fluorine-silicon compound. The different colors are the result of the admixture of various metals in the stone.

Where found	Urals, Sri Lanka, South-West Africa, USA and in tin mines in Brazil
Color(s)	dark yellow to golden yellow; white, silver, blue and pink varieties are found
Chemical composition	$Al_2 [F_2/SiO_4] + OH + (Cr, Fe, Mn)$
Hardness	8
Available forms	small rough stones, touchstone, cut in jewelry
Crystallization	topaz is an orthorhombic crystal prism with rich surfaces; the color is yellow through chromium, golden through phosphorus, brownish through manganese, and blue through iron

Tourmaline

History and legend

In antiquity it was believed that the stone glowed because of its own energy. The stone becomes electrostatically charged when rubbed.

Healing properties

Green tourmaline (verdilite) regulates the blood pressure and can strengthen the heart muscle and nervous system; it also stimulates the digestion and strengthens the immune system. Black tourmaline (schorl) can protect against high radiation, and has a positive effect on the locomotor system while strengthening the vegetative nervous system and musculature. Blue tourmaline (indocolite) combats water-retention, promotes detoxification of the body, strengthens the immune system, and reduces throat and bronchial infections. Watermelon tourmaline alleviates pain, strengthens the immune system and protects the nerve cells.

The name is derived from the Singhalese word turmali, *"different stone."*

Magical properties
It symbolizes wealth, friendship and love.

Chakra classification
Green, watermelon, pink and red tourmaline work on the heart chakra; black tourmaline works on the root chakra, and blue tourmaline on the throat chakra.

Star sign
Blue tourmaline is linked to Libra, green to Capricorn, pink and red to Scorpio.

Tourmaline was much favored by Biedermeier.

Application and care
Tourmaline is discharged once a month under running water and recharged by being placed in sunlight for a few hours. Pink tourmaline should not be charged in sunlight but in an amethyst geode.

Where found	Madagascar, Sri Lanka, Angola, Mozambique, South-West Africa, Brazil, USA, Pakistan, Afghanistan
Color(s)	colorless (elbaite), pink, red (rubellite), violet, brownish, dark brown, yellow (dravite), blue (indocolite), deep black (schorl), green (verdelite); also green, innen pink to red (watermelon); translucent
Chemical composition	$(Na,K)(Mg,Fe,Li,Al)_3 Al_6 [(OH,F)_4/(BO_3)_3/Si_6O_{18}]$
Hardness	7 to 7.5
Available forms	cut as a gemstone; small pieces are used as an amulet or healing stone
Crystallization	usually long, extended trigonal crystal prism, whose varying play of colors comes from concentrations of iron, manganese, calcium, nickel, cobalt, titanium, chromium or sodium

Pink and red tourmaline (rubelite) regulates the metabolism, detoxifies the body and stimulates the blood circulation. It has a stabilizing effect on the female sexual organs.

Tourmaline quartz

History and legend
In ancient China tourmaline quartz was known as a harmonizing stone, one which achieved a harmonious balance between the two poles yin and yang, the female and male principle, and heaven and earth.

Healing properties

Tourmaline quartz is rock crystal that has grown together with black tourmaline.

Tourmaline quartz is successfully used to treat disorders of the digestive tract and to detoxify the body. It develops its liberating power against negative energy most effectively in the form of a sphere. The stone is also very effective in the treatment of dizziness, pain of all kinds, and nerve injuries. Sciatica and lumbago can also be alleviated by tourmaline quartz. It is a harmonizing stone that promotes tranquillity and relaxation while reducing aggression.

Magical properties

Tourmaline quartz symbolizes unity. The stone belongs to the quartz family and envelops black tourmaline needles in transparent quartz.

Chakra classification

The stone is particularly effective on the secondary chakras of the hands and feet. It also works on the forehead chakra.

Star sign

Tourmaline quartz is linked to Capricorn.

Application and care

Discharge the stone among rock crystals or tumbled hematite stones and recharge in the sun.

Tourmaline spheres are particularly effective.

Where found	China, Australia, Brazil and Madagascar
Color(s)	like quartz, with black inclusions
Chemical composition	this stone has the composition of rock crystal with black tourmaline inclusions: $SiO_2 + NaFe_3(Al, Fe)_6[(OH, F)_4/(BO_3)_3/Si_6O_{18}]$
Hardness	7
Available forms	polished as a touchstone or for laying on the body; however it is most used for jewelry or as a tumbled stone
Crystallization	quartz, with black tourmaline inclusions; trigonal crystal

Tourmaline quartz is a member of the quartz family. It has particular mineralogical and geological properties as a result of its combination of rock crystal and black tourmaline.

Tree agate

History and legend

In India tree agate is perceived as a talisman. It is a very rare type of agate and therefore has no particular application. It is often combined with rock crystal to make rosaries because used in this combination it is believed that it deepens concentration and prayer.

Healing properties

The rare tree agate produces gentle vibrations and therefore has a calming effect on the nervous system of its wearer. In addition, it is said to stimulate the healthy functioning of kidneys and bladder, thus regulating the water balance in the body. It strengthens the immune system and powers of resistance of its wearer.

Tree agate is also thought to influence the psyche, encouraging perseverance and conveying a feeling of inner peace. It helps its possessor in his relationship with children. Combined with chryso-

The rare tree agate is found mainly in India and Australia.

prase it produces warmth and tranquillity. The stone reduces arrogance and egotism. It promotes the recognition that every-one is only part of a whole.

Chakra classification
Tree agate is a supporting stone. It is most effective on the heart chakra. Its powers are intensified when it is combined with a chrysoprase or ruby zoisite stone.

Star sign
Tree agate is associated with Capricorn.

Application and care
Tree agate should be cleansed regularly under warm running water. Necklaces should be cleansed overnight in a bowl with tumbled hematite stones. Recharge the stone in sunlight, then leave it to rest for one hour before using it again.

Tree agate is most effective when used in combination with other stones.

Where found	India, Australia
Color(s)	white tree agate with moss-like green inclusions
Chemical composition	SiO_2
Hardness	7
Available forms	rough stone, touchstone, sphere, necklace, pendant
Crystallization	trigonal crystal

The white tree agate with moss-like inclusions is a member of the quartz family. It owes its particular appearance to deposits of manganese and iron.

Turquoise

History and legend

Crusaders discovered this stone in Turkey, the country after which it is named. But turquoise had long been considered a holy stone by American Indians, who also believed it was a magic stone providing protection against harm. The objects discovered in ancient Egyptian and Greek tombs show that turquoise was also considered a protective stone in antiquity. It was used to protect both horse and rider on long journeys. In the Middle Ages it was thought to give women a sense of happiness and contentment and guarantee success and power to men. Hildegard von Bingen used it as one of the twelve fundamental stones in her naturopathic treatments.

Turquoise is a protective stone for travelers by air.

Healing properties

Turquoise is an effective treatment for a wide range of disorders: it helps in the treatment of throat and lung infections, and it alleviates

hyperpepsia and general stomachaches as well as rheumatism and gout. It cures infections, speeds recovery after illness, alleviates pain and reduces inflammation. In addition, it has antispasmodic and detoxifying properties. Psychologically, it lifts depression, gives self-confidence and promotes endurance.

Magical properties
Turquoise symbolizes beauty. In the Middle Ages it was believed that it made women virtuous and loyal.

Chakra classification
Turquoise is particularly effective on the throat chakra.

Star sign
Turquoise is linked to Aquarius.

Application and care
Discharge once a month in a bowl of dry tumbled hematite stones and recharge overnight among rock crystals (not in sunlight!).

The most beautiful specimens are found in Arizona.

Where found	Arizona, and also in Mexico, Tibet, Myanmar, China, Israel (where it is known as Eilat stone) and former Silesia, now Poland
Color(s)	light blue to turquoise blue
Chemical composition	$CuAl_6 [(OH)_2 / PO_4]_4 \cdot 4H_2O + Fe$
Hardness	5 to 6
Available forms	tuber-like pieces are found; worked and cut as a jewelry gemstone
Crystallization	an aluminum acetate phosphate, grape-shaped triclinic crystal, usually found in seams of aluminum-rich rocks in the neighborhood of copper mines

The stone stabilizes extreme mood swings and counteracts apathy. It gives new energy and makes one feel active.

Ulexite

History and legend
The stone was named after the Hamburg chemist G. L. Ulex (1811–83). It is also popularly called "television stone," because when the stone is cut in a particular way it works like a glass fiber cable: crystals contained in the stone convey an image of what the stone is resting on to its surface.

Healing properties
Ulexite has anti-bacterial and disinfecting properties. It also works indirectly as a prophylactic against the tetanus bacterium. In addition, it can be used to treat eye problems. Psychologically, it helps the wearer to make decisions. It also guides in the further planning of how to achieve a particular objective. It prevents its wearer from being too trusting and encourages greater realism. In addition, it improves the memory and willingness to learn.

Ulexite has a velvety white to grey translucent texture.

Chakra classification
Use ulexite on the secondary chakras of the hands and feet. For the other chakras it is used as a booster stone with other stones.

Star sign
Not linked to any particular star sign.

Application and care
Cleanse the stone once a month under warm running water. If used under the pillow, cleanse it twice a month by leaving it among rock crystals overnight.

The Indians also knew of the antiseptic properties of ulexite.

Ulexite is believed to be a prophylactic against the tetanus bacterium. The wound may be disinfected by placing the stone on it or bathing it with a ulexite infusion. That will neutralize the bacteria.

Where found	Nevada, Oregon, and California
Color(s)	white to gray, translucent
Chemical composition	$NaCa [B_5O_6 (OH)_6] \cdot 5H_2O$
Hardness	1
Available forms	sold primarily as rough stones
Crystallization	triclinic crystal, fibrous needles

Vesuvianite

History and legend
Vesuvianite was known in antiquity as a healing and protective stone. The ancient Greeks called it *idokras* ("mixed form"), but it is now called vesuvianite because it was first discovered at the foot of Mount Vesuvius. Both the Greeks and Romans knew and used the healing powers of this mineral-rich stone. It was one of the first stones to be ground into powder for healing purposes.

Healing properties

Vesuvianite develops its healing properties particularly as bath-salts and as an infusion.

Vesuvianite alleviates chronic illnesses caused by environmental pollution such as lead and mercury. It is therefore a very useful remedy in our modern civilization. It has a cleansing and purifying effect on the body and assists recuperation after a lengthy illness. It is also very beneficial to its wearer's psyche; it drives away fear and melancholy. It makes the wearer open to his environment and

292

stimulates his desire for action. People carrying a piece of vesuvianite cannot hide their feelings.

Chakra classification

Vesuvianite works well on the heart chakra. To harmonize and
strengthen your heart chakra, lie on your back completely relaxed
and place the vesuvianite in the middle of your chest. Close your
eyes and direct all your concentration to your heart chakra.

Star sign

Not linked to any sign in particular.

Applications and care

Discharge and cleanse the stone once a month under warm running water. Then recharge again among rock crystals for a few
hours.

Vesuvianite was known in antiquity as a healing and protective stone.

Where found	as the name suggests, it comes from Vesuvius in Italy; also: USA, former Soviet Union
Color(s)	from green through yellow to brown
Chemical composition	$Ca_{10}(Mg, Fe)\,Al_4\,[(OH)_4/(SiO_4)_5/(Si_2O_7)_2]$
Hardness	6.5
Available forms	as a natural stone and also as a crystal
Crystallization	tetragonal prismatic crystal, extended, quadratic cross-section

Vesuvianite or idocrase is a mineral-rich compound of calcium, magnesium and iron. That is why it has a particularly cleansing and purifying effect on the body.

Zircon

History and legend
In antiquity zircon was called "hyacinth." The name came from a mythological character, Hyacinthus, a youth accidentally slain by Apollo who was jealous of the young man's beauty. His blood produced the hyacinth flower whose beauty is reflected in the red variety of zircon.

Healing properties
Zircon has a wide range of healing applications. It has an anti-spasmodic effect on the liver and gall bladder. It has a calming effect on asthma and allergies and has a beneficial effect on lung infections and bronchial problems, severe colds and complaints of the respiratory tract. It also alleviates abdominal cramps caused by intestinal and digestive problems. It stimulates the metabolism and prevents water-retention in the tissues as well as the blood

Zircon is a stone that promotes peace.

pressure that would result from it. It alleviates pain, including menstrual pain and brings on late menstrual periods.

People who believe that they are too materialistic can be helped by a zircon.

Magical properties
Zircon symbolizes healing. It helps its wearer overcome losses, heals mental disturbances and promotes common sense.

Chakra classification
Zircon works well on the root and sacral chakras.

Star sign
Zircon should be placed in dry sea salt once a month, where it discharges and recharges again at the same time.

Applications and care
Zircon should be placed in dry sea salt once a month where it discharges and recharges at the same time.

Zircon can lower fever and reduce inflammation.

In cases of separation, zircon helps its possessor to let go and makes him aware of the transient quality of life. It promotes better understanding of reality and promotes dreams.

Where found	Australia, Cambodia, Thailand, Sri Lanka, Norway
Color(s)	colorless, yellow, orange, brown to violet, blue and green
Chemical composition	$ZrSiO_4$ + Al, Ca, Ce, Fe, Hf, P, Th, U, Y
Hardness	6.5 to 7.5
Available forms	as a natural stone for laying on the body, worked and cut for use in jewelry
Crystallization	four-sided prismatic crystal formed from island silicates, found in granite; tetragonal crystal

Zoisite

History and legend

Zoisite was only discovered in the nineteenth century. It was discovered in Austria and was named after the person who found it, Baron von Zois. It is a modern stone whose blue variety, tanzanite, was only discovered in 1967 in the vicinity of Mount Kilimanjaro in Africa. It was quickly made famous by the New York jewelers Tiffany. Since then it has become a highly sought-after gemstone.

Healing properties

Zoisite is beleived to be a kind of fertility stone that is effective for both men and women. It is also a protective stone for women during pregnancy. It is said to stimulate cell division, detoxify the body, and strengthen the immune system. However, the stone only works slowly. In addition, it promotes creative and constructive tendencies and is therefore helpful in the case of

Zoisite promotes growth and strengthens the immune system.

extended convalescence.

Magical properties
Zoisite symbolizes sexual desire, fertility, and good health in unborn children.

Chakra classification
It is most effective on the heart chakra because it harmonizes the heart and circulation of the blood with its gentle vibrations. It also works well on the root chakra.

Star sign
Not linked to any particular star sign.

Application and care
Zoisite must be discharged once a month under warm running water and recharged in sunlight. The blue stones are more complex and must be charged in a bowl of water among rock crystals and sapphires.

Elizabeth Taylor has magnificent jewelry set with blue zoisite.

Zoisite is normally green. The pink-colored variety of zoisite is called thulite, differing from the green variety in its high manganese content. There is also a blue variety, tanzanite, and a ruby zoisite with ruby inclusions.

Where found	exclusively in Tanzania
Color(s)	green, pink, blue
Chemical composition	$Ca_2Al_3\,[O/OH/SiO_4/Si_2O_7] + Cr, Mg, Sr, V$
Hardness	6.5
Available forms	small crystals are available, as well as tumbled stones; it is also used in the form of disks
Crystallization	it originates from the conversion of basic magmatite; orthorhombic or trigonal crystal

Your Personal ABC of Crystals and Gemstones

Organize your own home
pharmacy of healing stones.
Find the most important
stones at a glance and the
ailments they treat.

A Home Pharmacy of Crystals and Gemstones

Mild illnesses or those in their incipient stages can be cured through the use of healing stones. It doesn't matter whether their origin is physical or psychological. Use the healing power of nature. It is free of side effects; it does not lead to complications or other problems. And it is always available.

For those who suffer from recurring symptoms or chronic ailments a pharmacy of healing stones can be immensely helpful. All you need are a few precious or semi-precious stones. You might also want to put together a necklace especially tailored to your own needs. It can consist of stones that have a positive influence on a particular chakra or physical condition. Just as with tumbled stones, a personal healing necklace can be easily carried with you and can accompany you while traveling. In this way the most important stones for both you and your family can be in easy reach at all times.

A basic collection of crystals and gemstones is all you need to start your home pharmacy. Twenty or so should be more than sufficient. Not only will this be easy to assemble, the process can be most enjoyable. In addition to its practical benefits, your healing stone pharmacy will be an attractive addition to your home or office. Display it on a bookshelf or behind glass. Its aesthetic qualities will complement its therapeutic power.

The following alphabetical guide lists common physical and psychological disorders and will help you find the corresponding gemstones to treat them. Please be advised that stones' effects will not be felt overnight. They do not work miracles and are not a substitute for a doctor's care.

Abscess Tape amber onto the affected area, and leave it on day and night until the abscess is gone. Rose quartz helps soothe the pain.

Acne A paste made from soapstone should be left on the skin for a few hours. You can carry rhodochrosite as a touchstone. Every night you should wash with aventurine water, made by placing the stone in rain or well water for a day. Women should wear jewelry made from aventurine.

AIDS Stones cannot work miracle cures. But they can strengthen the immune system. Amber is effective worn directly on the skin. A man can wear it in a flat necklace underneath his shirt. This will help the immune system. A tourmaline necklace can also be worn.

Allergies The best defense against allergies, including hay fever and allergies to animals, is amber in tumbled form as a touchstone or worn as jewelry. Also pearl, aquamarine, beryl and zoisite are helpful. Hyacinth and turquoise work to calm allergic symptoms. Preventing allergies: if someone who is allergic to animal hair visits a dog or cat owner and his eyes start itching and tearing, quick help can be found by wearing an amber necklace.

Anemia For chronic anemia a necklace of beads made of hematite should be worn next to the skin. This needs to be discharged each night under running water.

Anger People who fly into rages against those around them or when things don't go their way, should wear or carry objects made from silver. This will help stifle anger.

Angina Disks of beryl and aquamarine should be placed for a half an hour each day on the throat chakra. For symptoms of longer duration one should wear a short turquoise necklace.

Anomie Apatite and/or carnelian will help you recover your interest, when you feel passive and cannot summon up any initiative. Often they will help you find courage for new undertakings.

Anxiety Malachite, rhodonite and turquoise should be worn. Place tourmaline on the heart chakra. For free-floating anxiety a necklace of aventurine is recommended. For anxieties related to specific situations, job interviews for example, pyrite can be carried as a touchstone.

Arthritis One should wear amber in any form whenever possible. Malachite also yields good results. It is important that the stone has contact with the skin.

Asthma and respiratory disorders One should wear amber, tiger's eye, zoisite, falcon's eye and prase. One can also drink or bathe in malachite water.

Backache Apply pyrite. Amber or obsidian can be worn as jewelry. Those suffering from backache should consult a physician since back pains can signal more serious conditions.

Balance, impaired sense of No matter where the problem comes from, the sense of balance will be improved by the use of tourmaline, agate and emerald.

Bedwetting An uncut piece of rose quartz should be placed on the floor lying about three feet from the bed.

It should be discharged once a week under running water.

Bladder infection For acute cases one should drink one half-gallon of nephrite water every day. For chronic inflammation wear heliotrope and also place it directly on the bladder for half an hour a day.

Blisters, caused by burns Immediately place rock crystal or carnelian on the affected area.

Blood pressure For high blood pressure: Wear or carry sodalite. Before bed, place sodalite on the forehead chakra for fifteen minutes. Wear jewelry made from lapis. Chrysoprase is also helpful. For low blood pressure: Wear amethyst and ruby. Caution: Patients with low blood pressure should not wear lapis!

Blood sugar, low Mornings and evenings lay red brown jasper on the navel for fifteen minutes. Also place the stone in a glass of water overnight and drink it the next morning on an empty stomach.

Boils Apply amber as long as boils are not open. You can also tape it overnight directly on the boil.

Bones, ailments affecting To promote healthy bones in children: chrysocolla. For osteoperitis in older people: coral. For pain: labradorite. For general strengthening of bone: apatite, smoky quartz, amber. In each case the stone should be applied for half an hour. In the case of chronic or severe pain a stone can be left on the problem area overnight.

Breast feeding Chalcedony worn regularly while nursing promotes the production of milk in young mothers.

Bronchitis Wear amber and in the evenings rest a piece of pyrite on the breastbone — especially for chronic bronchitis. For jewelry tiger's eye is recommended. Please note that jewelry should lie directly on the skin. Wear fashioned stone. Touch it frequently.

Bruises Place or tape amethyst to the affected area.

Burns, minor Immediately place chrysocolla or rock crystal to the affected area.

Cancer For grave illnesses such as cancer or AIDS stones cannot offer miracle cures. That said, one must strive to support the body's own healing power. To that end it is recommended that a chain of small black or various-colored tourmaline be worn. Always carry a touchstone made from sugilite. Lapis lazuli can be worn with good results in the early stages of the disease.

Circulatory disorders Best is to wear either amber, turquoise or garnet.

Colds Aquamarine can be worn or carried. Lay pyrite on the body.

Concentration Confused thinking and lack of concentration can be ameliorated by wearing amethyst. It promotes clear thinking. Those with mentally demanding occupations should drink amethyst water in the morning on an empty stomach.

Connective tissue disorders Wear smoky quartz or carry it as a touchstone.

Constipation For acute constipation: place a tumbled stone of red-brown jasper in a glass of water overnight. Drink the water on an empty stomach. Wear beryl or topaz. Place carnelian on the stomach.

Cramp Drink zoisite water and wear or carry zoisite as a touchstone.

Creativity, lack of Wear a chain of nephrite every day. This will stimulate and develop your creative powers in all spheres of life.

Cysts A stone of black tourmaline should be applied to the affected area or tape carnelian onto the stomach overnight.

Depression A chain with tourmaline should be worn. Tourmaline is especially helpful for those going through a change of life. Amazonite should be placed on the heart chakra or worn as an amulet. Lapis lazuli has long been recognized as protecting against depression of all kinds; it has a calming influence when the soul cries out for help. Kunzite, tiger's eye and turquoise (good-size pieces) can be carried as touchstones.

Diabetes Place a disk made of citrine or pyrite on the third chakra every night for half an hour. Also lay a disk of moss opal or moss agate right next to the pancreas.

Diarrhea Drink beryl water several times a day.

Discontent Pearls are helpful for those who feel unable to make the best of the circumstances in which they find themselves. Especially recommended for older people

Disk pain Wear rock crystal and lay it upon the back for 20 minutes under a red light (see also "back pain", "sciatica" and "lumbago"). Consult a doctor to determine the underlying cause.

Disorganization Aquamarine answers to the need for organization in your life, thoughts and emotions. It will also help you finally straighten up your desk.

Dizziness Those prone to dizziness should wear a fine chain made of red, green and pink tourmaline. Emerald can also be used in the chain. They should also drink agate water.

Energy, lack of Jasper gives new energy to those who feel sleepy and worn out. It helps its possessors to embark upon new undertakings.

Envy By wearing a chain of small pieces of olivine one can counteract the tendency toward reacting to others with envy.

Exhaustion For some weeks every morning drink diamond water on an empty stomach. Wear or carry coral in any form.

Eye ailments For poor eyesight: A small piece of emerald may be placed at the corner of the eye or glued to an eyeglass frame. Wearing rock crystal, beryl and chrysoberyl is also helpful. For inflammation: Wash the eyes with onyx or emerald water (use a clean fresh cotton cloth). Agate, apatite or rock crystal can be placed on the eyes. For cataracts and glaucoma: place rock crystal directly on the eye three times a day.

Fertility Where there is no inhibiting sickness, the woman should wear a necklace made from jade, red jasper, moonstone, smoky quartz and rose quartz. This necklace should be left overnight in a glass of water and in the morning both partners should drink it before eating.

Fever At the onset of fever one should immediately put on a necklace of amber. Disks of agate, chysocolla or jade should be applied to the heart or forehead chakra.

Gall bladder Red-brown jasper is good for ailments affecting the gall bladder. It can be applied as needed directly on the area around the gallbladder. Rose quartz, either rough or polished, is also helpful.

Gas Every evening before bed lay a pyrite or citrine disk upon the navel chakra for twenty minutes and place a red-brown jasper disk next to it.

Gastritis Pyrite or red brown jasper

should be placed on the stomach for fifteen minutes directly after eating. If that is not convenient, wear an amulet made from either stone on a leather thong long enough to reach the stomach area.

Gout Amber and/or turquoise are recommended. In the morning, drink diamond or topaz water on an empty stomach. If diamonds are used, make sure that they are kept in the water for at least twelve hours prior to drinking.

Grief and loss Zircon and amazonite can help you cope with the loss of loved ones and go through the grieving process.

Gums, inflammation of Rinse the mouth regularly with amber water. After using, recharge the stone in sunlight.

Hatred When the soul is darkened and full of hatred, one should turn to chrysocolla. This stone eases, calms and slowly dissolves hate.

Hay fever From January until the end of July, wear amber on a chain. For other healing stones see "Allergies".

Headache Excellent results can be obtained by wearing a chain of amber. This even works for migraine. Other stones that alleviate headache include amazonite, amethyst, falcon's eye, lapis lazuli, pearl, rose quartz, emerald and tiger's eye.

Hearing disorders Place onyx or black tourmaline on the crown chakra for fifteen minutes in the morning and evening. Hearing loss: as soon as this becomes noticeable place onyx on the ear for fifteen minutes mornings and evenings. For buzzing or ringing in the ears: tape a bit of tourmaline below the ear and leave for half a day. Do this for ten days. If there is no improvement, consult a physician. Stones will not remedy the problem.

Heartburn Wear silver jewelry or a chain of turquoise. Apply pyrite or malachite. Drink turquoise water.

Hemorrhoids Drink hematite water three times a day.

Hepatitis Red-brown jasper and pyrite heal hepatitis. These can either be carried as touchstones or placed directly on the body.

Homesickness One who suffers from homesickness or separation anxiety should always have beryl nearby.

Immune system For a weak immune system an amulet of labradorite should be worn directly on the skin for at least half a year. If there is a genetic disposition towards cancer, one should wear lapis lazuli jewelry. For general strengthening of the system, olivine, green tourmaline and ruby should be placed over night in red wine (jewelry made from rubies can also be used); in the morning drink the wine in small sips.

Impotence Every evening apply rough ruby, red jasper, garnet or rhodonite onto the root chakra.

Inflammations Place spinel or compresses soaked in spinel water on the affected area. For inflammation of the ovaries: Place carnelian on the abdomen every night.

Inspiration, lack of; writer's block Blue topaz and sodalite help with a failure of creativity. These stones stimulate fantasy and new ideas.

Irritability Gold topaz helps lessen irritability in one's day to day life and counters the tendency to get worked up about small things.

Jealousy Jealousy can be mitigated through the use of diamonds and black tourmaline.

Joy of life, lack of Amber and

hematite strengthen one's capacity to discover and enjoy the beautiful things that life has to offer. They are most effective when held as touchstones. They will help you find the joy in living once more.

Kidney ailments Jade should be worn for all kidney problems. At night place a jade chain in water along with hematite and drink in the morning on an empty stomach. Nephrite can also be used.

Labor During pregnancy the expecting mother should always wear malachite, carnelian and jade in no matter what form. During labor carnelian strengthens the mother's reproductive organs. Jade helps stop bleeding during and after birth.

Laryngitis Wear chalcedony, blue topaz or aquamarine.

Legs, tired and swollen Hematite, amber and chalcedony are best worn together in a necklace.

Lesions For acute cases: wear amber. For chronic cases: leave some peridot in olive oil for two weeks. Then apply this solution directly onto the lesions morning and night.

Liver ailments Use red-brown jasper and rose quartz as touchstones. Topaz, citrine, tiger's eye, moss opal, epidote and amber can be laid on the body.

Love, pain of For the one who suffers love's pangs or is beset by the grief of loss and separation, rose quartz and malachite can offer some comfort.

Lumbago A piece of flat smooth amber should be taped to the painful area of the lower back. Carry it until the pain goes away.

Lungs, disorders of Olivine, pyrite and rhodonite strengthen the lungs.

For acute inflammation wear or apply turquoise or drink turquoise water.

Lymph system For swollen lymph nodes or to stimulate the lymphatic system, wear or apply aquamarine.

Marital fidelity Spinel will keep you faithful to your partner and help you avoid temptation.

Memory, weakness Garnet jewelry should be regularly worn. It strengthens the power of recall.

Menopause Drink yellow jasper water every morning. Wear coral or moonstone with blue tourmaline. Place pyrite on the navel chakra at least a half-hour before retiring.

Menstrual problems Lay pyrite on the painful area for twenty minutes a day. For regulating and stabilizing fluctuations in hormones, it is best to wear pearl and moonstone. Very good results are obtained by placing a flat piece of malachite a hand's breadth below the navel during one's period.

Mental clarity Those who always need to keep a clear head should use heliodor (a form of beryl).

Metabolic disorders Amber stabilizes the metabolism. Citrine stimulates it. Rhodochrosite, pyrite, topaz, zoisite, moss opal and moss agate are all helpful.

Migraine Amber is the most effective treatment for chronic recurring migraine. It should be worn for a considerable length of time. Best is to wear a short flat necklace that will not disturb one's sleep. Migraine caused by stress can be alleviated by rhodochrosite or tiger's eye. Use them to lightly massage the temples in a circular motion.

Moral sense From the earliest times, jade has been known to sharpen the sense of morality and justice. Beads of rock crystal are also helpful, as is azurite.

Multiple sclerosis Serious illnesses such as MS, cancers or AIDS always call for a doctor's care. Healing stones can support medical treatment and, above all, summon the patient's soul power to meet their challenges. It has been repeatedly confirmed — as with cancer and AIDS — that wearing a chain of tourmaline can slow the advance of the disease or even halt its progress altogether.

Muscle ailments For muscular weakness: rose quartz and black tourmaline. For inflammation: amber or obsidian should be taped to painful area.

Negative thinking Chrysoberyl can help those who always imagine the worst.

Nervous disorders Nervousness: citrine, pyrite, sapphire, all kinds of topaz, moss agate and moss opal. Iolite is good when used as a touchstone. For inflammation: wear a chain made from amber alternating with tourmaline. Sodalite can be used as a touchstone.

Nightmares These can often be prevented by wearing heliotrope to bed. Chalcedony is also effective in combating anxiety-filled dreams. Or you can place an uncut piece of rose quartz next to your bed. This should be discharged once a week under running water.

Obesity Place red-brown jasper overnight in water and drink in the morning on an empty stomach. Then let the stone stand in the sun all day to recharge its energy.

Pain Aventurine, dioptase and kunzite relieve pain. Rose quartz is good for those who suffer from headaches and sore eyes after working at a computer for long periods of time.

Paralysis When paralysis affects one side of the body, as is usually the case in victims of stroke, one should, as an addition to standard medical treatment, wear a necklace of tourmaline. At night one can use an amber necklace in its place. Both necklaces should be short, small and flat, so that they don't irritate the patient.

Parkinson's disease Wear a chain of tourmaline. It can at the very least supplement standard medical treatment.

Phobias Every kind of phobia, whether fear of spiders or elevators, will be eased by rhodonite.

Pregnancy, difficulties during Malachite, jade and carnelian ought to be worn during pregnancy. Agate and heliotrope will help when you feel unwell.

Psoriasis Place a small stone of olivine in olive oil for two weeks, then dab the oil on the affected areas morning and evening. You should also wear amber.

Restlessness Amethyst and aquamarine work against restlessness. One should apply pyrite to the third chakra. Amazonite should be worn to provide a sense of inner peace. Prase is useful when worn as an amulet or applied to the body. Use labradorite as a touchstone. Sapphire jewelry has a claiming effect.

Rheumatism One should bathe in hot sapphire water twice a week. Amber can be worn in a necklace or as an armband. Labradorite and sard are helpful when placed on painful areas.

Sciatica As with lumbago a small piece of amber should be taped to the point from which the sciatic nerve issues from the spinal column and where the pain is most severe.

Self-esteem, low To increase self-esteem, wear chalcedony. Gold is also helpful. Best is chalcedony set in gold.

Sexual problems Garnet and rubies should be worn. They help both men and women. One can also use rhodochrosite and red jasper to massage the area below the navel.

Shingles Wear rose quartz and place amber mornings and evenings on the affected areas.

Skin disorders Soapstone cleans; moss agate water calms inflammations; aventurine and rhodochrosite help blood circulation and regenerate the skin. Onyx makes skin soft and smooth, but it only takes effect slowly.

Sleep disorders Best results æ especially for restlessness in young children — come from placing a piece of rose quartz, at least 3" in diameter, on the floor next to the bed. This must be discharged once a week. A small, narrow band of hematite placed on or around the neck overnight relaxes and promotes good sleep. Amethyst can also be used to good effect.

Sore throat For laryngitis: gargle with chalcedony water. For infections, wear a necklace of turquoise, lapis or chrysocolla.

Sorrow Apatite assuages daily sorrows as well as those arising from difficult circumstances. These can strain the nervous system. Small everyday sorrows, jealousy, problems in love, can rob life of its joy. Don't let them get the better of you. Use healing stones to protect yourself and regain the sense that life is worth living.

Stomachache Of psychosomatic origins: malachite should be worn. For digestive ailments: carnelian and red-brown jasper are to be worn. Let smoky quartz lie directly on the stomach for fifteen minutes. Menstrual cramps: wearing carnelian or placing fire opal or fire agate on the painful areas can be effective.

Stomach and intestinal disorders To promote regularity: beryl. Against inflammation: wear or apply red-brown jasper and take either moss opal or carnelian water — best is to drink a glass over the course of a day. For ulcers: red-brown jasper helps in any form, topaz can also help.

Stress Place a small piece of rock crystal directly on the skin. Stress that results from overtaxing oneself can be eased by wearing jewelry made from chrysocolla. In situations of extreme stress a disk of red jasper or pyrite should be placed directly on the third chakra for thirty minutes. For those who have an exaggerated reaction to normal stress, smoky quartz can be very helpful.

Stuttering Those who stutter, especially children, should always carry pyrite with them to use as a touchstone.

Suicidal thoughts Someone who has suicidal thoughts should immediately seek out a qualified psychotherapist. In addition, citrine should be worn, ideally in a necklace against the skin.

Tension Tension arising from anxiety, suspicion and anger is dispersed by the dissolving rays of topaz.

Thyroid All light blue stones work equally well to stimulate the thyroid; they also can have a calming effect. Recommended are chalcedony, aquamarine, bright blue lapis, sodalite, blue topaz.

Tonsillitis Wear or apply amber. For chronic recurring tonsillitis a chain consisting of chalcedony, turquoise, sodalite, aquamarine and blue topaz should be worn over a long period of time. Use small stones to make up the chain.

Travel, fear of For two days before departure carry beryl as a touchstone. Once you are on your way switch to kyanite.

Tumors By placing sard directly on the tumor in its early stages, one can retard or stop its growth.

Varicose veins Wear a band around the leg (not too tight) consisting of smooth amber, hematite and chalcedony. Drink hematite water on a regular basis. Hematite can also be placed directly on affected area while keeping the legs up.